LIFE COMPASS:
FINDING YOUR TRUE NORTH

Xulon Press
2301 Lucien Way #415
Maitland, FL 32751
407.339.4217
www.xulonpress.com

Paperback ISBN-13: 978-1-6628-5037-0
Ebook ISBN-13: 978-1-6628-5038-7

When I met Dr. Donald R. Hudson in 1995, he provided me with much-needed spiritual direction. His book, *Life Compass: Finding Your True North*, can do the same for you! It is a powerful and practical tool you can apply to your unique life journey. What I love most about this piece is Dr. Hudson's willingness to be transparent. He models the same *admitting, accepting,* and *acknowledging* in which he encourages his readers to be engaged. Sit back, soak this in, and let it change your life!

– Rev. Joel A. Bowman, Sr.
Founding Pastor, Temple of Faith Church, Louisville, Kentucky
Licensed Clinical Social Worker/Freelance Writer/Poet

Life presents many twists and turns that present opportunities of how we could allow life to twist and turn us (literally and theoretically) or how we can and should control the twists and turns to navigate each step towards our True North. Should you or someone you know be situationally obstructed, uncertain, or unaware of next steps, metaphysically barred from putting plan(s) into action, taking a deep introspective dive into *Life Compass: Finding Your True North* will foster the directional shift presently needed. Be patient, open to receive, and open to implementing the information and instructions saturated on each page. Navigating through life will be different for each person. Still, obtaining a grasp of one's True North sets the tone for each step crafted in the navigational system of your life. Your True North is yours. Allow this book to offer you a path of how to find and maintain focus of your True North.

– Exceptionally Based
(City: True North, State: Life)

In reviewing *Life Compass: Finding Your True North*, I find it to be true to fact. We can find ourselves in a cage or become complacent in the so-called box we've put ourselves in and have become accustomed to. We can get so caught up in the worldly aspects of living that we forget to do the building up of self on the inside. I love the passage in this book about how one's inner sanctum is private and sacred, and if we fail to nourish that private place, we can become lost within ourselves. I think this book is a great read and guide for all of us in "Finding Our True North." Doctor Hudson, you hit the nail right on the head. God Bless you, sir.

— **Stephond Ward**
Private Nurse/MHT (Mental Health Technician)
Dallas, Texas

Reach your potential and find self-fulfillment by discovering and following your inner compass. This is the message Dr. Donald Hudson gives us in this powerful, keenly insightful, and creative book, *Life Compass: Finding Your True North*. You will learn how to map out the path to reach your divinely designed destiny by living a compass driven life. This book is a treasure that will bless you on this journey now and years to come. No matter where you are, just follow your compass. It always leads to the point of fulfillment.

— **Dr. James C. Perkins**
Pastor, Greater Christ Baptist Church
Detroit, Michigan

Pandemics of various sorts abound as many are left holding shattered pieces of their past and broken pieces from the life that they had imagined. Nothing is the same. Dr. Hudson seems to feel the angst of our culture and the restlessness of our soul quietly asking, "what now"? He so poignantly and powerfully challenges us and chorales the reader to pick up their pen filled with the ink of disappointment, desperation, and despair and begin authoring a new story. "Finding Your True North" is first an inward journey before it is anything else. Dr. Hudson's compassion, care, and transparency are so beautifully prevalent throughout this book. One can sense his urgency and desire that the reader turns North and finish their story. This book is a must read!

– **Dr. Genetta Y. Hatcher**
Senior Pastor, The Room Church
Detroit, Michigan

With skill and aplomb, Dr. Donald R. Hudson gives us a book that is a frabjous read and guide. There is a Ciceronian elegance to the 'Prompts." Which makes logical and spiritual encouragement to action. Hudson sedulously guides us in finding our True North with actionable steps one can take to produce a result of great use, or service. Finding our True North, Hudson helps us see means by which we can give thanks each day. We can live each day with hearts bursting with appreciation. We can start and end each day with gratitude, till gratitude isn't what we choose, it's who we are. Hudson's book is remarkable and remarkably relevant.

– **Dr. Michael Walker**
Appreciation Financial
Dallas, Texas

Life Compass: Finding Your True North is a delightful guide full of valuable information for those of us who want to improve your self-care. I am talking about finding your very own True North. The author gives you that inner sense of what you want to accomplish in life. That calling which keeps you on the right track to being your authentic self.

– **Ka'Mili Grayson**
Published Author & SKST Radio Podcast Hostess
Virginia Beach, Virginia

Dr. Donald Hudson is to be commended for acknowledging his vulnerabilities to excavate this gem and guide readers toward their True North. *Life Compass* is a map that leads to fulfillment of an authentic life vision without influence or distraction. It is a must-read for anyone who dares to embrace a life fueled by distinct magnetic force – their true *Life Compass*.

– **Dr. Norman E. Freeman, Jr**
Senior Pastor
Greater Antioch Baptist Church
Pompano Beach, Florida

In my line of work, hearty conversation and sound counsel are the two main and active ingredients of my workday. Truth is most people come to my office or reach out to me for a video or conference call when they are in a troubling predicament or some form of crisis. My job then becomes focused on getting to the root cause of the issue. To do so, it requires getting to the true essence and heart of the individual's thoughts about what occurred and their role in the issue. It is in those instances of unearthing the authentic True issue that a plausible solution and/or gameplan can be developed and deployed. I find that individuals seeking to have better outcomes and results in their work-life are those that are honest and who are willing to do the work to remain True to themselves. As a certified coach and human resources professional, I am ecstatic that Dr. Donald R. Hudson has penned *"Life Compass: Finding Your True North."*

This body of work is necessary. Individuals endure a lot of ups and downs in this life, but the ones that overcome are those that seek to tap in and understand themselves at a deeper level to arrive at their place of destiny, i.e., their True North.

I highly recommend this work to individuals and groups inside and outside of the workplace. This work is not just another surface level self-help book. This work requires the reader to seek truth and dig for deep understanding. Dr. Hudson provides us with Compass Prompts that will get anyone reading this work started on the journey of True North self-discovery. This work will help me in counseling individuals at my place of work. I'm certain it will help you too. Get your copy today!

– **Harriett E. Johnson, MBA**
Director Human Resources
Certified Coach

LIFE COMPASS:
FINDING YOUR TRUE NORTH

Admitting Your Past, and Accepting It
Accepting Your Present, and Owning It
Acknowledging Your Future, and Going for It

Dr. Donald R. Hudson

Foreword by **Kevin Dudley, PhD** and
Eugene Cowan II, MDiv.

XULON PRESS

To my awesome beautiful wife Leatrice. You live life with faith and within the power of the possible.

To our awesome unique daughters, Zuri, and Zenobia. You take the path of your uniqueness out loud and in the light.

To our awesome granddaughters, Amari, and Skylar. You are growing into your ownness.

To my sister Alice Betts. My last surviving sibling. You continue to display what it means to remain determined to reach your destiny. You live your life out loud and with faith.

To those of you who have discovered that the path of life sometimes consists of maddening mazes, with no light at times, but you keep going, stumbling at times, and sitting down at times, walking, and running at other times, but you are still going for your true destiny without apology.

And to those of you who have yet to identify your path and may not have a clue as to what your destiny is, I also dedicate this book, because your path awaits you and your destiny is waiting for you to show up.

To you, I dedicate this book.

Writing New Stories and Shaping New Experiences

It is not where a person comes from that determines the rest of their life. I believe that our lives are determined basically by how we decide to handle the present, and by what we honestly expect in the future despite our past and go for what we expect.

We cannot change our history. Yesterday has been etched in the stone of time and cannot be erased by any means or effort. Whether our past is negative or positive it remains what it is, and we must accept it.

However, our present is like a fresh sheet of paper that can be written on, or like fresh clay which can be shaped. If we use our present whether negative or positive to write new stories and shape new experiences, we can compose and shape our future into something great. Therefore, we must choose wisely as to how we use our present – our "now." It can be wasted, or it can be wonderful. Writing new stories and shaping new experiences is a matter of choice. We have been granted creative powers to change things and redirect the course of our lives. It is ours to be the author of our stories and the sculptor of our future.

– Dr. Donald R. Hudson

Table of Contents

PART 3
Accepting Where You Are, and Owning It

PART 4
Acknowledging Where You Want to Go, and Going for It

Acknowledgements

The idea for *Life Compass: Finding Your True North* was conceived and crystallized as I challenged myself to take an in-depth look at my life journey and as I considered the journey of others.

This book challenges us to take a deep look at ourselves and accept who we are and release the person we are created to be. We are challenged to live aloud and in the open while knowing that life has much more to offer than what we have already experienced. It reveals how we are wired as well as to why we are wired the way we are. We are wired the way we are for a purpose and for a particular destiny that only we can fit.

I felt compelled to author this book because as I consider my own story, while considering the stories I have heard from others, I concluded that our stories are similar. They just unfold on distinct stages in life and in different theaters in life and at various times and we play the leading role. Nevertheless, we all have a story that is connected in some way or another, that makes up the path of our Life Compass that is intended to lead us to our destiny. Therefore, I have written this book.

My words cannot express my deep appreciation for the special people who encouraged me to write this book as they shared their own stories and beliefs about what they believe following our compass means. Some of the people who encouraged me to pursue the idea of this book had no clue that the words and wisdom they imparted to me fueled the fire in my belly to dare write a book of this nature that each of us can relate to in some way or another despite our condition of existence.

From the moment this book was conceived, there were people who stuck with me to make sure that this literary work would get out of my head and heart and onto the pages of this book and released. They inspired me in their own unique way to continue the path of my Life Compass.

Deep gratitude goes to my wife, lover, true friend, and partner, Leatrice Hudson. Thank you for your editorial acumen, as well as for your limitless support as I take the path of my compass and pursue my own destiny. Thanks, babe, for being by my side through the thick and the thin as you held on in the curves and twists in the journey.

Thanks to Harriett Johnson-Williams for being my Advisor and Project Manager from the very start of this book project. You stuck with me even when the ideas of this book were written on napkins. Thank you for helping me order my thoughts about Life Compass. Thanks for pushing me to stay on track. Your tireless dedication will always be appreciated.

Thanks to Eleanor Graves, the wife of the late Bishop Michael Graves and the Proprietor of the Graves Memorial Library in Durban, South Africa. Thank you for your unending wisdom and passionate support as my Writing Coach. Thanks for being a friend and mother to me and for believing in the message of this book, as well as believing that I could write this book. Your encouragement and insight will never be forgotten.

Thanks to Pastor Eugene Cowans, III, the CEO of EC2 Ministries. Thanks for being an awesome son in the ministry, as well as a genuine friend. From the conception of this book project, you believed in the message of this book, and you believed in me.

You continued to encourage me to stay the path of writing this book. Your ideas and input for this book have helped me remain focused on its purpose.

To each of you, no matter the role you played in my life as I pursued the completion of this book, I am grateful for you. You are awesome. Much love and thanks to you all as you take the path of your own Life Compass and reach your True North.

Most of all, I offer my deepest thanks to God my Creator for life and for giving me the chance, mind, and heart to write this book.

Foreword

This is a really good book!

It is rare in our contemporary world that is unapologetically preoccupied with empty soundbites, cheap attractions, and idiotic arguments to find a wise communicator who can share thoughtful and meaningful perspectives that can make a transformative difference in our lives. Dr. Donald Hudson is such a voice so desperately needed today.

Dr. Hudson has tapped into something powerful and wonderful with the "Compass" metaphor and his insistence that we claim our "True North." Though we have "the way," we are not always successfully able to "find our way" for a host of reasons. The reader is invited to confront the areas of interference and distraction on the journey with honest introspection, strategic emphasis, and uncompromising commitment through an engagement with the very practical instruction outlined and explained here.

The circumstances and conditions of our lives are certainly important to consider. The unforgiving realities of our daily existence reveal that the way has never been easy. Yet, Dr. Hudson reminds us that the longings and stirrings of our purpose and passion, which reside deep within us, are the critical elements that essentially dictate our response to the promise of "life to the full" continually unfolding before us.

At once refreshing, challenging, and encouraging, the thoughts shared in this work help the reader to chart a decisive path to experience the fullness of the life she or he has always intuitively and instinctively known to be present. This is the universal calling to be true to whose and who we are. No more excuses. No more delays. No more defeats. It will be difficult not to be inspired by the guidance of Dr. Hudson's timely words.

-Dr. Kevin Dudley
Senior Affiliated Professor of Church and Society
Trinity Lutheran Seminary at Capital University
Columbus, Ohio

Foreword

Dr. Donald Ray Hudson for me has been a Pastor, Mentor, Father, and most of all a friend. As I reflect on our relationship, I speak to the authenticity of who he is as a person. He shares his insights from his life experiences and pulls back the curtain to display the magnet that keeps him grounded which is the Creator and his own humanness. I am deeply honored to be able to share my gleanings from "Life Compass: Finding Your True North."

Life Compass allows you the opportunity to reorientate yourself to the map of your purpose, vision, and values. It allows you the space for grace because we have been conditioned by culture and not seeing the brilliance of God's working in our life amid crisis and trauma. What gets us off track or what detours us from our destiny is distractions. This book is about reflection, resilience, and personal restoration from life's distractions. Dr. Hudson shares the purpose of a compass which is to tell you the path to take as it is orientated to your life. The magnetic pull of the compass is that Intuition, Instinct, Inspiration, and Inclination of the spirit that sets us on course to discover our destiny.

Life compass is about being conscious, deliberate, disciplined, and intentional about your path. It is about pursuing your passion with purpose. Along this journey, you discover more about yourself and more about the Creator who is guiding you. Dr. Hudson shares about solitude and the value it brings to the journey. Many of us cannot handle the salvation of solitude because we suffer in silence and the space feels the same, but it is not. In solitude is where you calibrate your compass and your map, it is the planning, it is making sure you're still headed to your destiny.

-Rev. Eugene Cowan II, DMin
Chaplain & Senior Pastor New Light Full Gospel Baptist Church, Virginia Beach, VA

Prologue:
A Note to the Reader

I started thinking about life compassing several years prior to beginning to write this book. Much of my delay at starting to put the ideas and concepts in book form was due to my lack of understanding the necessity and the importance of living a compass driven life. I have heard of being purpose driven, but not compass driven. I made it my business to make honest attempts to live with purpose. I finally came to conclude that both purpose and compassing go together. Purpose is the reason for which something or someone exists. It is about intended or desired results. I discovered that even though one may have an idea of his purpose, he may not have discovered his path on which he lives out his purpose.

Prior to putting pen to paper, or should I say, putting fingers to computer, I had a fairly good idea of what my purpose was. However, the path which I was to take to live out my purpose was not always clear. Therefore, some of the paths I took while attempting to live out my purpose did not match my purpose. As a result, I got lost on the journey like we all do at times.

When I started writing this book it was during one of the most crucial times in the world's history. It was the time of the COVID-19 pandemic that took the world by storm. In the United States, many people lost their jobs and had to consider other careers or means to make a decent living. This caused many people to get lost and work hard at getting life back on its true path. During this time, I came to realize that living compass driven was something that we need. Without it, we would meander through life without reaching the destiny for which we are created.

I hope that you will be encouraged by the words printed on these pages. The words you read have been pinned from the deep inkwells of my life journey. Some of these places were painful and painted with disappointments. Some of the pain, I must admit was self- inflicted, while others were totally out of my control, or simply by life occurrences. Some of these places were fun, funny, and rewarding, for all of which I am grateful and thankful to the Creator.

The words and thoughts composed in this book were birthed out of the dawning of new days as I began to redefine myself, write new chapters of my life and challenge myself to take the path for which I am created. They were also birthed out of the sunsets of days, as I discovered and came to the reality that I must be intentional about positive change. Such intentions impressed upon me to end chapters of my life that were no longer suitable for the next level of my life, as well as for the path that I was created to take.

I have learned through this course of life whether negative or positive, whether in want or wealth, or whether at the hands of others or life circumstances or at my own hands, that if life is going to be fulfilling and exciting – yielding those experiences that may be deemed deeper and meaningful and full of purpose. I had to learn to pray over, and over again for something bigger than myself and not settle for merely surviving through life. This has not been an easy task to perform.

Through this portion of my life journey, I have learned that we should look for what we believe to be true through the eyes of our hearts, even if it takes a while to see it with our physical eyes. We must learn to live by faith and not simply by sight.

We should develop the courage to face the facts of our lives, fight for something bigger than us and expect to win. It takes faith, courage, effort, determination, and the will to live and keep our truest path. This is not easy. But it can be accomplished.

This book has been written with deep concern for the pains, disappointments, struggles, and difficulties that sometimes paint the canvas of human existence.

I hope that something said in this book will encourage you to hold on tight and not give up. I pray and hope that you will discover or rediscover your truest self and truest life for which you have been created to live without shame or apology. Live your life out loud and in the open for the world to hear and see. I believe that when we make honest attempts to embrace our Life Compass and to be determined to live accordingly, our "Impossible becomes our I'm-Possible."

FROM THE AUTHOR

Introduction:
The Journey

W elcome to Life Compass: Finding Your True North. I am happy and excited that you are joining me on this awesome and sometimes unpredictable journey called life. If you are reading this book, it is not by happenstance, nor accident. You are hereby divine providence. You are ready to take your true path that leads you to the place of a fulfilled life without props. If you have picked up this book, the unique you – the authentic you, who has been caged, is calling out to be released and set free from the various bondages that have kept many of us from living the life we deeply desire to live. I know that it is sometimes hard to admit that there are times when our lives get off track, we find ourselves stuck in some rut where we are just spinning our wheels and going nowhere, and if we are going somewhere, it is not fast, rewarding, or empowering.

Such reality can be a shock to our ego system, particularly when we have arrived at a place in our lives that we deem successful. You know those places that paint the picture of success based upon the societal definition of what success is supposed to look like. You know what I'm talking about – the lean body, the big house, two to three cars, awesome vacations once or twice a year, the big paycheck (*money in your pocket*), children in college with tuition paid, expensive restaurants, staying in suites at four to five star hotels, clothes in the closet with tags still on them, you are highly educated, popular (*everybody is calling your name*), you got a good family (*even though some appear to be a little to the left*), you raised smart and productive children, you got the position. All these things are a perfect picture of what success is supposed to look like from the lens of society, (*there is nothing wrong with having things when they are kept in proper perspective.*) Then one day you hit the wall of reality. You discover that while you were busy building your success story, you did not spend much time building yourself, your inner sanctum.

Our inner sanctum is that private and sacred place of our existence. It is the deep place of our existence where we make decisions that informs us how to approach the world. Our inner sanctum is our core. Our core is the central, innermost essential part of our lives. When we fail to nurture and strengthen our core, we often lose ourselves in the hustle and bustle and we get thrown off our intended path. If this is your case, do not be hard on yourself, because it happens to the best of us regardless of our position in life. It is a part of real life. You are not alone. We are on this journey together. Our stories are not that much different, they are just played out on different stages, in different places, and at different times. The hard part is facing our reality.

Why this Book?

Several years ago, my life collapsed around me after having built a life that many people would consider successful. I must admit that I have been very blessed and fortunate to have lived a comfortable life, with all the bells and whistles. But underneath all of that, my life was collapsing. I suffered in silence. Many of my days in the light were spent in the dark. Sounds familiar?

No one knew it because I mastered concealment. I was busy encouraging others and ignored the need to encourage myself. I was busy helping others keep their life on track to the point that I lost myself and my truest path. The collapse that I experienced had less to do with me losing things, versus it being caused by me losing myself in the hustle. The hustle of trying to prove to people that I was alright and that I was successful. I discovered that even though others deemed me as being successful and had it all together, I lost myself along with my truth. In many cases, you can never tell a book by its cover. In the words of the great hymn of Christendom, written by John Newton, *Amazing Grace*, "Amazing Grace, how sweet the sound, that saved a wretch like me, I once was lost, but now am found, was blind but now I see." I admit without shame or apology, that there was a time amongst my successes, I was lost and blind to my truest path and settled for going in directions that did not fit me or them. This was often because instead of living out my truth and my authenticity, I resolved to attempt to live a life that was measured and defined by what society classifies as a happy successful life. Do not get me wrong, there is absolutely nothing wrong with having an aspiration for good things and success, but they must not be what defines us, neither should we depend on them to make us happy.

After careful consideration and prayer as it pertained to where I was in my life at that time, I resolved that to get my life back on track I had to come to grips with the fact that I was lost, and I had to do something about it. So, I decided again to come into a real awareness of my own authenticity. This time I approached it without relying on the props to define my worth and value, or people to make me happy or feel good about myself. After carefully thinking about how I ended up in some maze and off of my true path, I came to the conclusion that perhaps if I was feeling this way, there are others who are experiencing the same type of feelings or something similar and needed to know that they don't have to live the rest of their life in some maze and that they can get back on their true path. They are not alone and can rediscover themselves. If we take the time to stop, look and listen, we will discover that we all have a story that is painted with negatives, positives, pain, possibilities, setups, and setbacks that makes up our path. The path is leading to a wonderful destiny.

I was reluctant to write this book because there are times when it is hard to face one's own realities. However, I discovered during the process of self-rediscovery, that making the decision to face our reality whether bitter or sweet, lacking, or productive, is one of the healthiest, and empowering decisions we can ever make. Facing our realities tells us where we have been and where we are, and if used correctly and learned from it, it can inform us of the correct path to take as we move into our future. As I was writing this book, I became more and more convinced that no matter what our position is in life's journey, each of us can lose our way and ourselves from time to time, and we need somebody to remind us that it is okay and that we do not have to remain in the state we are in. So, my friend, I offer you to join me as we take the journey through, "Life Compass: Finding Your True North." Welcome. We are in this together.

Who Should Read this Book?

Who should read this book? You should. This book has been written for the millions of people regardless of where they are in your life journey. It has been written for those who are ambitious, determined, and intentional about achieving everything that is possible for them. It is also written for the millions of people who are just starting to get a grip on life, and for those who may not have a clue as to where they want to end up in life, or exactly what they want out of life. Finally, it has been written for those who are in a season of changing the direction they go, for the remainder of their life. Each of us fits in at least one of these categories. This book has been written for everybody regardless of the season we are in on our life journey and desire to live the best life we can.

For us to live out our uniqueness for which we have been created and gifted to do, we must be willing to accept our truth without shame or apology. When we accept our truth, we accept our flaws, as well as the things we are good at and have accomplished over time. Such acknowledgment of our truth helps us discover or rediscover the path that leads to our destiny. Of course, this takes self-development and self-discipline. Without self-development and self-discipline, we will not stay on the path of our life compass which helps us to stay on our truest path, and we resolve to take the road of least resistance.

This book has been written as a self-help book and as a guide to help you to become the remarkable person you are created to be.

What This Book Is Not About

This book is not about how to make more money, even though once you begin to live according to your life compass and find your North, you may discover that you already have the abilities and potential to produce wealth or become more innovative in managing the wealth you already possess. Living according to our Life Compass puts us back on our truest path and to be more aware of ourselves, as well as to what we already have at our fingertips. I contend that when we lose ourselves in the hustle and bustle, we mismanage our lives. When we mismanage life, we usually mismanage the other things in our lives, such as finances, time, family, and our giftedness. When we are off track everything in our possession gets off track.

This book is not necessarily about success theories or formulas as it pertains to society's definition of success. Rather, you will be given the opportunity to rediscover what success means to you from your own perspective and definition. Our success should not be based upon someone else's definition, or what they deem is successful, even if it is appealing to us. Success means different things to different people. When we attempt to be successful from someone else's perspective, we usually get off track to what is meaningful to us.

Finally, this book is not a fairytale or a sugarcoated version of life's journey. Life is real and can be bitter at times. In this journey we call life, we get lost and end up facing dead ends, twists and turns. Then, on the other hand, life can get so off track, and all we seem to have been given are pieces that do not connect – mess.

What This Book Is About

This book is about being committed to a path. We will never reach the pinnacle of our lives without staying on our true path. Our highest point in life is reached when we can finally live a joyful, satisfying life that is not dependent upon props. I define props as those things or people we depend on to be happy or satisfied. When we no longer have possession of these things, or the people we depend on for our happiness, or for our satisfaction betray us, our lives seem to fall apart and get off track.

This book is about rediscovering ourselves or being deliberate and intentional about cultivating who we are authentically. Each of us gets to a point in life where discovering who we are is most important. We all have the tendency to lose ourselves, even while making a good living. Being lost is when we no longer feel inner joy and peace. This causes us to take paths that do not lead to our truest destiny. On the other hand, when we do not cultivate our authenticity, we have the tendency to spend time and energy, attempting to cultivate and develop someone we are not. This book is about reinventing and redefining ourselves as we follow our Life compass that leads us to our True North. I will speak on the idea of True North in the following pages. If we are going to live our lives in their truest sense, it is important that we practice reinventing ourselves. As we move throughout life, there are times when it becomes imperative that we take inventory of who we have become, as well as where we are in life. I contend that once we take the time to take a self-inventory, we discover new things about ourselves. Self-inventory helps us identify what no longer works for us, as well as discover new life practices that we are not aware of.

Reinventing ourselves does not necessarily imply that something is out of order. It simply states that we have discovered a need to be different than before and to do things differently. Self-inventory also helps us redefine ourselves. We all have had experiences that tend to define us. Self-inventory helps us look at ourselves deeper than our experiences and circumstances. When we take a self-inventory, we tend to discover that we have the capability of doing more and accomplishing more than what we have done and accomplished before. Each of us can do more and accomplish more.

This book is about getting back to our truest self, after having realigned with our "Life Compass and having identified our "True North." I will define "Life Compass" and "True North" in the following pages. Let us face the fact, that with all the demands of life, such as careers, family, paying bills, trying to maintain our health, attempting to find personal time, along with the various issues of the world, we tend to lose sight of ourselves, as well as what is important to us. I am not suggesting that we push these things to the side because they are important. I am suggesting that these things must be placed in their proper perspective to give us room to see ourselves in our truest form. The only way we can be true contributors to the world in a positive manner, we must do so from our authenticity. We cannot be positive contributors to the world when we have lost our authenticity. If we are attempting to live outside of our authenticity, we end up spending time and energy trying to fit into what does not fit us, or us it. It is about not trying to force what does not fit, versus finding where we fit and what fit us, so that we make positive contributions to the world as we live our lives in their truest form.

Finally, in a nutshell, this book is about knowing and accepting where you have been without shame or apology. We all have a past, whether pleasant or unpleasant. Our past cannot be changed. Our past is etched in the stones of time and cannot be erased. Though our past cannot be erased, we do not have to live the rest of our lives patterned by it.

The best that we can do with our past is to learn from it. When we put our past, whatever it is, we can use it as part of our Life Compass that can propel us towards our True North. It is also about honestly knowing and accepting where we are in our journey. This too, should be done without shame or apology. I must admit that knowing and accepting where we have ended up, can sometimes be a hard pill to swallow, because we have imagined ourselves being in other places, doing something different than what we are presently doing. If we are honest, many of our lives do not presently resemble the picture we painted of the life we desire to live. If this is your case, lighten up and do not be so hard on yourself, because each of us gets off track from time to time. It is just a matter of deciding to get things back on their proper course. It is also about knowing where you want to go.

Knowing where we want to go is most important. When we fail at being honest about where we want to go, we will end up anywhere. When we fail to identify where we want to end up in life, we have the tendency to settle for whatever life throws at us or attempt to live according to what others think is good for us, for the mere sake of survival. Living in survival mode often causes us to take the road of least resistance, and we miss living according to our passion and purpose. In a nutshell, this book is about being who you are and embracing you, all of you, and loving you, as you follow your compass and get to the place in life for which you were created. This makes life worth living and more enjoyable.

The Benefits You Can Expect

Once you have committed to your truest path, rediscovering, and owning your authenticity, through deliberate and intentional pursuit, and boldly taking the chance to reinvent and redefine yourself despite your past or present circumstances, whether your circumstances are productive or lacking, you will begin to embrace your awesomeness and uniqueness out loud, and in the open, for the world to hear and see without apology.

As you take the journey through this book, you will gain a fresh perspective of who you are, and that will help bring you into the light of your life journey. You will develop a new mindset concerning the various events and episodes in your life, whether negative or positive. You will learn from the pages of this book, that every experience we encounter in life has a purpose, and they all fit together one way or another, and that such experiences are not for our destruction, but for our development into the person, we are created to be. These experiences help make up our Life Compass that leads us to our Truest North.

Furthermore, you will learn to trust your instincts and own them, even if others do not necessarily agree with your decisions as to how you choose to live your life, and what you choose to keep or let go out of your life. Choosing to live according to your instinct, as well as make decisions according to your instincts will give you a fresher perspective and respect of yourself, and therefore you will get a fresh perspective of others, as well as respect them for the decisions they make for their lives, even if you do not agree with them. Of course, this is a learning process within itself.

How this Book is Written

In the pages ahead, you will discover that this book is divided into four main sections which makes it user-friendly. I also use affirmations throughout the book that I hope will inspire you. In this book, I offer pieces of my own story that I contend will help you arrive at the conclusion, that there are times in each of our lives when we lose ourselves in the hustle and bustle of life's journey and that we should not be ashamed because life has greater possibilities, regardless of where we find ourselves presently. At the end of each section, I offer you space for journaling. Journaling has played an important role in my life and has helped me get back on the path I am created for, as well as helped me identify my True North. I believe it will do the same for you.

Part I is entitled *"What is Life Compass."* In this section, I describe what a compass is, as well as what I mean by Life Compass as it pertains to our life journey, and the important role it plays, as it relates to us living and traveling our true path that leads to developing and maintaining an enjoyable life full of potential, by which we are empowered to achieve everything we are created to achieve. I will also describe in this section what I mean by True North. I will offer ways to discover your True North, as well as ways to arrive at your True North. In addition, I will talk about the Magnetic Pull, which is a part of the compass. I will give a description of what I mean by Magnetic Pull, as well as offer you ways in how to connect to it, as well as its importance as it pertains to living according to your Life Compass, and how it helps us move towards our True North which is our destiny. I will also talk about being intentional about making the necessary changes to be compass driven.

Part II is entitled *"Admitting Where You Have Been, and Accepting It"* In this section, I talk about facing our past failures and mistakes. I will address the subject of "Facing the Facts" – the facts of our lives. The fact is, we all fail at something, and sometimes at the things we are good at. I contend that when we do not face our past failures and mistakes, they can dictate our next level of life. If we are not intentional about breaking the chains of our past failures and mistakes, they tend to cause us to regret our past to the point that we punish ourselves which cause us to not bounce back from our disappoints, and we begin to measure ourselves by others, and their accomplishments.

Therefore, in this part of the book, I will expound upon the fact that our failures are not final. Because we fail at something, it is not the end of our story. I will talk about how our failures can work for our benefit. I will encourage you not to punish yourself because of your past, and how to bounce back from your disappointments, as well as not measuring yourself according to others and their accomplishments, but instead, measure yourself according to you.

Part III is entitled, *"Accepting Where You Are, and Owning It."* In this section, I deal with the importance and necessity of being clear as to where we are presently in our lives. If we are not clear about where we are presently, we fail to embrace our uniqueness and spend too much time and energy attempting to do and cultivate those things that do not fit us or them. I contend that when we fail to grasp the reality of where we presently are, we have the tendency to go in no certain direction. Not knowing where are, can be confusing and stressful, because we steadily attempt to put together pieces that do not fit, nor reveal a clear picture of who we are. I admit that having clarity of where we are presently, can be somewhat disappointing, because it may reveal that we have been wasting time at being a fictional character, versus being the real us, or we have been spending time living a life for the satisfaction of others, versus for the satisfaction of ourselves. Furthermore, when we fail to identify where we are presently, we fail to release our awesome authenticity. Therefore, in this part of the book, I will address subjects such as Self-Clarity, Life Detoxification, Self-Inventory, and Realigning with our Life Compass. Each of these subjects are imperative if we are determined to live our lives according to our Life Compass that leads to our True North, which is our truest destiny.

Part IV is entitled, *"Acknowledging Where You Want to Go, and Going for It."* In this section, I deal with the importance and the necessity of at least having some idea of where we are going and where we want to end up in life. No matter who we are or what type of life we have lived in the past, we can choose the type of life we want to live presently, and in the future. However, if we do not have an idea of where we are going and where we want to end up in life, we will end up anywhere, and it is usually, places we do not want to be.

In this portion of the book, I deal with how to use your imagination to help follow your Life Compass and get to your True

North. If you cannot see yourself somewhere other than where you are presently, chances are you will remain where you are. Also, in this portion of the book, I encourage you to "Just do It." The idea of us just doing it is about going for what you want out of life. However, going for what you want is not without risk. If there is no risk involved in what you are trying to accomplish, what you are attempting to do may be too small for your potential. In addition, I encourage you not to settle for nesting. Do not resolve to simply stay where you are and become comfortable with doing what you are doing for the sake of making a check and making ends meet when you have much more to offer and the potential and promise to do more. Instead, dare to take a leap into your unique presence and into your awesome future.

In the concluding chapter, I expound upon the 7Cs that are the basic principles of this book, as well as what I believe can be the basic principles to live a compass driven lifestyle.

Welcome to Life Compass: Finding Your True North!
Get ready! Your best journey is about to begin!

How to Use this book

This book is composed of four parts and sixteen easy to read chapters. In the appendices, I give you "Compass Prompts" based upon each chapter in the book which are actions exercises that will assist you as you take your Life Compass journey. I suggest the following four steps that will help you get the best out of this book:

Step One: Schedule some quality time in your favorite space. I suggest reading this book in a quiet place if possible while listening to soft music or with nature sounds. But choose what is best for you.

Step Two: Read this book with something to write with so that you can make your own personal notes as you read, or just write in the margins of the pages. I found this to be helpful while reading because it allows you to record your fresh and natural thoughts about what you are reading.

Step Three: As you read this book do so with an open mind and heart concerning yourself and your life journey. Do so while imagining your life changing for the better full of possibilities.

Step Four: When you reach the conclusion of this book, schedule some time to engage in the Compass Prompts provided for you in the Appendices. The Compassed Prompts are based upon certain major points from each chapter. They will help you along the path of your compass as you are directed to your True North.

AFFIRMATION #1

I am not an empty vessel. I awake each morning full of potential, talents, and power that enable me to be successful and add positivity to others. I came into this world with a purpose and a rewarding destiny.

Part 1

What is Life Compass?

If we are not deliberate about going in a certain direction, or at least pointing in the direction we desire to go, we are lost. If the essence and quality of life are contingent upon anything other than our inner peace, authentic joy, and soulful rest that does not depend on props, our compass is off, or we are off our compass, and we can end up anywhere. Everyone is born with a Life Compass. It is called intuition, instinct, and gut feelings. When we embrace our Life Compass, we will always be pointed in the direction of our True North which is our destiny. We will reach our destiny when we pay attention to the inner spirit that drives us and pulls us in the direction we should go.

Chapter 1

Living Compass Driven

*"Set the compass in yourself by what you know deep within,
and without compromise, like living by that."*

-John De Ruiter

Everyone needs a life compass that helps keep them on the path that leads to their destiny. Whether you are currently living within the perimeters of your ideal life, or finding yourself meandering in some valley of indecisiveness, or resetting your life, or have simply settled for where you are in life.

Every person born into this world has been born with a purpose, regardless of your current position or status. And you can live according to your purpose and arrive at your destiny when we follow the path of our inner compass. The difference is that some people discover their purpose and arrive at their destiny sooner than others because they have come in tune with their inner compass. The fact remains that we all have been born with a unique destiny on the inside of us that desires to be released into the world out loud for the world to see and hear. **Unfortunately, there are those who never discover their purpose or destiny. The good news is that you are not one of them. You can know your purpose and your destiny. It will take some thought, changes, and some work,**

1

<u>but you will get there.</u> Even though we all have been born with a destiny, it is not automatically reached.

Our destiny can be defined as that which we have been created and naturally equipped to accomplish. It is that place in life at which you arrive that gives you a sense of joy and belonging. It is that place that once you arrive there, you feel good because you feel connected, and you can use your natural abilities to accomplish something that makes you feel good about yourself and about life.

If you are to release your destiny into the world, for it to be seen and heard, you must know it will not occur by happenstance or by luck. Neither is it kept undercover and in silence by the negative events you encounter in life or by bad luck. Your destiny is released for the world to see and hear when you follow your inner compass.

When you are intentional about following your inner compass, the negative events you encounter, or what some may consider as bad luck can only slow you down or detour you from your path. But, when you are intentional about living a compass driven life, you are lured back to the path of your compass and in the right direction that leads to your destiny, even though you take bypasses from time to time.

To live compass driven we should have some type of understanding of how our compass operates, as well as to how it connects to our everyday life as it pertains to staying on your true path and reaching the destiny for which we are created. So, let me offer you an idea as to how a compass works and how it can help you stay on the path and reach your destiny.

What is a Compass and how does it Operate?

A compass is an instrument used for navigation and orientation that shows direction relative to the geographic cardinal direction.

The diagram called a compass rose shows the direction north, south, east, and west on the compass face.

When the compass is used, the rose aligns with the corresponding geographic direction. For example, the "N" mark on the rose points northward. Compasses often display markings for angles in degrees in addition to the rose. North corresponds to zero degrees, and the angle increase clockwise, so east is ninety degrees, south is eighty degrees, and west is 270 degrees. These numbers allow the compass to show magnetic North azimuths or true North azimuths or bearing.

If magnetic declination between the magnetic North at latitude angle and longitude angle is known, the direction of magnetic North also gives direction of true North. A compass always points to the magnetic North or true North. The needle of the compass always points North, because of the magnetic ring inside the compass. So, even if you are lost or get off track, you can always know where your North is. Then it becomes a matter of changing the direction you are traveling and heading towards your North.

When it comes to direction, true North never changes, despite how off track we get. The earth's magnetic field causes a compass to point North, as the compass is powered by magnets. The magnets inside a compass are drawn to the magnetic North.

What is Life Compassing?

<u>Life Compassing is living intentionally according to a personal plan and strategy, that if followed will heighten your possibilities of reaching and accomplishing your goals, objectives, dreams, plans, mission, and what you envision that allows you to embrace the destiny for which you are created.</u> With faith, determination, intentionality, hard work, and courage, you will

eventually reach the destiny for which you were born if you follow your life compass.

Life compassing is about staying true to your path. By following your life compass, you will stay on the path that leads to a more enjoyable life. <u>The enjoyable life you discover as you journey on your true path is not dependent upon the material, versus it being based upon the fact that you have arrived at an understanding that the quality of life is more about the fact that you have been afforded opportunities to connect with creation by which you are connected to the Creator, whose existence is not dependent on the material.</u> Even though living according to your compass is not always an easy task to accomplish, it is possible. Your quest should be to stay within the flow of your life compass to have an enjoyable life that makes life worth living.

Your compass is a natural intuition, instinct drive, and gut feeling that guides you down the path for which you are created and gifted. <u>Your Life Compass can be described as the map or path you follow that heighten your possibilities to reach and accomplish your goals, objectives, dreams, and plans.</u> This does not mean that there will not be times that you will not get off track. Getting off track is not the worst thing that can happen. However, never knowing your compass can be one of the worst things because you will remain lost, even in your accomplishments, and never arrive at your truest destiny. Even if you get lost, or off track, your compass helps you get back on the path to your purpose in life. Life Compass is about knowing and owning where you have been, knowing and owning where you are and knowing where you want to go.

There are times when we can get off track of our compass. If we are honest, we can admit that there are times when the picture we have painted for ourselves as it pertains to how we believe our lives should look, does not resemble the picture we painted. This is a part of life. Sometimes our lives do not resemble the picture we have painted because we failed or are failing at living our lives, according to our compass. If your life is not where you planned for it to be, or resembles the picture you have painted, for whatever reason, you are off your compass. But do not be discouraged, because each morning you wake up is another chance to make life into what you want it to be.

Living according to your compass takes focus, time, faith, and confidence, while you are going towards your destiny. Regardless of what happens around you, or the circumstances you find yourself in, once you get on your compass, you begin to go in the direction of your destiny.

I have discovered in my own life that it is not our compass that is off, it is usually us who get off our compass for some reason or another. I have also discovered that being lost can be most frustrating. It causes us stress and anxiety, and we fail to tap into those abilities, potential, and powers, as well as those opportunities that can lead to the possibilities of a better and rewarding life for which we are created to live.

Life Compassing is important because without it, life will go in any direction it chooses to go. Without deliberately directing life in a certain direction, the flow of our lives usually goes in a direction that is usually not healthy, empowering, or rewarding. Because of the many negative variables that exist in the world, life usually never flows in a direction that is powerful and promising. Life never goes instantly towards what is right or what is right for us. It usually flows in the opposite. When we do not live deliberately by our Life Compass, we never arrive at a place of our liking – the places we find the most joy or those places we planned to arrive at that embrace our purpose – our place of destiny.

Without a Life Compass, life starts to take on an identity of its own, without your permission. Your life becomes invaded by anything, and usually not by something you like. Without a Life Compass, your life begins to be shaped into something that does not resemble who you have been created to be. You take on the likeness of something you do not want to face each morning in the mirror. Therefore, discovering your Life Compass and going for your True North is important. I will deal with True North in the pages ahead. When you get off your compass, life can take avenues, streets, alleys, and by-passes, that cause you to settle for less than what you have been created for, or previously experienced.

We exercise life Compassing as a lifestyle and not as a one-time thing. It is a continuum. We exercise life Compassing by doing the following:

Admitting where we have been and accepting it. This can be painful, but one of the most empowering and liberating things we can ever do to get us going in the direction we need to go to get our destiny. Everything created with purpose starts from somewhere. Our personal history regardless of its particularities is our departure point which leads into the next phase of our life journey. Admitting and accepting our history no matter how far back or recent it may be, or how negative or positive it may be, helps us know what we are carrying on our journey, which can either be helpful or prohibiting. We will never get to where we are purposed to be without first facing the facts of where we have been.

Accepting where we are and owning it. Accepting where we are and owning it is about coming to grips with the person we have evolved into, as well as where we are in life. This includes new values, dislikes, strengths, as well as weaknesses and taking ownership of them. This allows us to plan our compass journey accordingly. If we do not accept where we are and own it, we may miss some valuable things about ourselves that are needed for the journey. It is also about being present in the moment. If we are not present in the moment, we will either stay connected to our past and spend countless hours gazing into the future that will cause us to miss doing what is needed in the present to get to our destiny.

Acknowledging where we want to go and going for it. No one arrives at a place without first having some type of clue or idea of what that place is. When we know where we are going, we tend to look for signs that indicate that we are going in the right direction, or in the wrong direction, or not moving at all. It is like traveling by automobile from one city to another. If there are no indicators that you are closer to your destination, it may imply that you are off your intended course or have resolved to stay still. We exercise Life Compassing by constantly keeping in mind where we want to arrive at in life, and plan and act accordingly. When we know where we want to go it helps us to not take paths that do not lead to where we desire to arrive.

In 2014, I ran across the book entitled "*The One Thing,*" written by Gary Keller and Jay Papasan. The book deals with the importance of discovering the one vital thing that one can pursue and accomplish, that leads to developing a successful and enjoyable life. I read the book from cover to cover and was impressed by its content, but I really did not get the importance of "The One Thing" until 2017, when I hit a wall in my life journey.

For more than a decade, I had pastored several churches successfully in several major cities in the US, but suddenly on one strange day in 2017, I discovered that things were not working out according to the picture I had painted. I came to the realization that for all the education, dedication, and hard work I had put in, I was caught in the current and flow of what others deemed as a success. Even though I was successful according to societal norms, I was failing inwardly, because I was not living according to my life compass, and I was feeling as if my real world was falling apart, while my outward world resembled an almost perfect picture.

I came to the realization that if I am going to live the life I was created to live, I had to rediscover my life compass and deliberately get back on the path that would lead me to a place in my journey that would enable me to embrace who I am, as well as my destiny. I came to the realization that this would take me to narrow my path. If you are going to embrace who you are, as well as the destiny for which you are created and gifted, and to live it out, it will take you resolving to narrow your path.

Narrowing Your Path

One of the best routes to take towards your destiny is the narrow path. Everyone has the same number of hours in a day. On average, everyone is afforded twenty-four hours, 1,440 minutes, and 86,400 seconds. So, why do some people seem to get more done during an average day than others? How do they seem to do more, achieve more, sometimes have more than others, and even seem to live a more meaningful life, when we all have been allotted the same number of hours?

I contend that those who seem to get more done, achieve more, sometimes have more, have much to do with the fact that they have resolved to narrow their path. We will never arrive at the place for which we are created, as well as to accomplish what we are gifted to achieve, without narrowing our path. I am reminded of the Scripture, Matthew 7:13-14 (NIV) that says, "*Enter through the narrow gate. For wide is the gate and broad is the road that leads to destruction, and many enter through it. But small is the gate and narrow the road that leads to life, and a few find it.*" Even though there is a spiritual side to this Scripture, I believe that it also informs us of the importance of narrowing our practical lives. The Bible is both spiritual and practical.

As I review my own life, I discover that much of my stress involved not taking the path for which I was created, as well as not using my potential to the fullest, because I was living an extremely broad life that could have led to my destruction in some way or another. Please understand, that when I say destruction, I am alluding to being overly stressed and full of anxiety and not being focused on my destiny, because I was involved in so many things that I thought were vital at that time. They could have been, but not always to my advantage. Destruction does not always mean physically. When we do not narrow our path, we run the risk of killing our dreams, passion, and productivity, because we get so involved in things that do not match us, as it relates to what we have been created for.

In a world of multiple choices, we must choose the route we take, even if it is not popular. We should consider narrowing our path, particularly if we are going to have a clear vision of ourselves and live a productive life.

A man or woman without a clear vision of self and life, tends to live a loose life that can sometimes become cluttered. On the other hand, a man or woman with a clear vision of themselves and the type of life they desire to live takes a narrow path, which simplifies their life. Narrowing your path does several things as it relates to being compass driven.

9

Narrowing your way allows you to know the direction you are created to go, as well as choose to go, and know which direction not to take. When you take a narrow way, you create space in your life that allows space for you to identify who you truly are created to be, because you are no longer hidden by the clutter. When you narrow your way, you lean more towards quality than quantity. When your way is narrowed, you do so by doing several things. You become very selective as to what you entertain, as well as what you allow to entertain you. I have learned that we cannot entertain everything or every opportunity that comes our way, even though some opportunities seem good, and stay on our path. Every good opportunity may not necessarily be good for us, depending on our destiny. We must pick and choose what opportunities are good for us and be deliberate and intentional about living according to our life compass.

When you narrow your path, you narrow your crowd. Proverbs 12:26 says, *"A righteous man is cautious in friendship..."* (NIV), and Proverbs 27:17 says, *"As iron sharpens iron, so one man sharpen another."* (NIV) When you narrow your path, you become very selective of the persons you make your company with, whether in person, virtual, or via conversation. This takes courage, because as you take inventory of those who are in your company, as well as those you have grown up with, you may discover that you have outgrown them, and they have outgrown you. There is no longer a fit. This is alright because everything and everyone must change.

When you narrow your path, you are careful about the words you speak and even the conversations in which you engage. Your words have power to either add life to your expectations or kill your expectations as you follow your compass. Proverbs 18:21 says, *"The tongue has the power of life and death, and those who love it will eat its* *fruit.*" (NIV) Even the conversations you engage in can help you stay the path of your compass that leads to your destiny or cause you to abandon your path. You are not just what you eat, you also become what you speak, as well as what you allow others to speak into you. Many of us are off our path because we speak the negative into existence, or have allowed negative conversations to influence our thinking, by which our actions follow. I am reminded of the Law of Attraction. The power of the universe does not just respond to our thoughts, but also to the words we speak, and the words spoken into us. People who have narrowed their path and have discovered their destiny as they do their best to follow their compass, are conscious of the words they speak and the conversation in which they engage.

When you narrow your path, you direct your energy and actions towards the things that really matter. When your path is broad, you tend to disperse your energy and actions towards things that have little or nothing to do with where you are trying to arrive at in life. This is not suggesting that you do not find time to engage in some fun events that do not take deep thinking. Even though you are serious about making life work at its best, you should also make time to relax and have fun with family and friends. But when it comes to following your compass, you should make it your business to put your energy and actions towards those things that are most important.

Narrow Your Options

As you narrow your path, you must also be willing to narrow your options to get the best out of your compass journey. You can't take everything offered to you and get to your destiny.

11

What are you choosing? It is not always what happens in your life that has the greatest impact on your personal world. Sometimes it is the choices you make concerning what happens in our personal world. It is sometimes the options you choose that make the biggest difference. Whether a situation is favorable or not, you have options as to how you choose to respond. You have the option to let what you experience make you, and you have the option to take your experiences and use them for something better.

One of the best gifts you are afforded is the gift of options. Having options is having the power or right to choose. What an awesome gift to have! I love the fact that we live in a world of many options. **No matter our skin color, race, culture, gender, or our beginning, we have options, even if we must make them ourselves.** One of the worst things you can do to yourself is to convince yourself that you have no other option but to let life be as it is. No person is without options. Sometimes you must dig for them or work hard as hell to make them for yourself. Even though having options is an awesome gift, having multiple options at your fingertips can be detrimental if they are not used properly or prioritized.

You can never get the best out of life or reach your authentic destiny when you attempt to take hold of every option presented to you, even when the options presented to you are good. I know that this may sound strange considering that we have been taught and encouraged to take advantage of every good opportunity that comes our way. Some of us were not taught the importance of prioritizing them or how to prioritize them. As a result, many people attempt to go for it all. When you try to go for it all you tend not to take hold of either. **We cannot say yes to everything presented to us no matter how good it is. Sometimes we must say "No" to some good things that come our way to say "Yes" to the better**

and the best that come our way. Even when it comes to options, there must be trade-offs.
When I look back over my life, I was afforded many good options. Even though I was afforded many good options, I contend that I missed some of my best chances to be elevated because I attempted to grab hold of every good thing that came my way. I was taught and encouraged to go for it all. I was not taught that to get the best out of life, I had to take the time to prioritize even the good things. Even though I made the decision to narrow my path, I was attempting to say "Yes" to everything good that came my way. While I was saying "Yes" to every good thing, I was not saying "Yes" to the better and best things. I later discovered that as I was narrowing my path, it was important for me to narrow my options as well. Narrowing our options helps us maintain the direction of our path.

When you do not take the time to evaluate your options or narrow them, several things can happen. Here they are:

You can become frustrated. The frustration comes because you are attempting to do everything, but you cannot do everything because you are one person.

Everyone's opinion of you and what you are doing begins to matter. When everyone's opinion begins to matter, you tend to pattern your lives to satisfy them.

You take on the mindset that everything must be done now. This results in you not getting the most important things accomplished.

You tend to get stuck at just being good or good at something. When you get stuck at just being good or simply good at something, you tend to never shoot for better or best.

13

In his book entitled, *Essentialism: The Disciplined Pursuit of Less*, Greg McKeown states the following, "... having fewer options actually makes a decision "easier on the eye and the brain," we must summon the discipline to get rid of options or activities that may be good, or even extremely good, but that gets in the way. Yes, making the choice to eliminate something good can be painful. But eventually, every cut produces joy – maybe not in the moment but afterwards, when we realize that every additional moment, we have gained can be spent on something better."

Here are ways you can narrow your options:

+ Make a list of your options.
+ Evaluate your options, and determine how do they complement your present and impact your future in a positive and powerful manner?
+ Prioritize your options from good to better to best.

Facing Mountains and Valleys

As you narrow your options as you follow your compass, you will be presented with the option to choose between Mountains and Valleys. No one can make this choice for you. It is inevitable that you choose. If you do something, you have made a choice. If you decide to do nothing and remain neutral, it is still a choice you have made.

No matter if you discover your Life Compass and begin living accordingly early in life or later in life, you must still choose whether you take the mountainous route or the valley route.

The valley route is easier to take, but not without its own obstacles. The mountainous route is a more difficult route to take. One year when I traveled to Congo Africa to engage in a mission effort to the Congolese people, one of our excursions was at the top of one of the mountains. As we made our way through the postcard scenes in the valley before reaching the top of the mountain, I was full of excitement, because I imagined that if the valley is this awesome the mountain view would be off the chain.

As we stood at the foot of the mountain my excitement grew. However, by the time I went the first five miles up the mountain, my excitement grew less due to the pain I was beginning to feel, as well as when I arrived at the conclusion, that taking the mountainous route to the village would require more energy and effort than it did going through the valley. This did not include the fact that I was given the option to take a jeep to the village, or simply remain in the valley. However, I continued to take the mountainous route. I discovered that choosing the mountain caused for more commitment, and energy to keep moving forward and upward to reach the peak. So, it is with living according to our compass. We have the option to choose between mountains and valleys.

In valleys, you can just walk through them with more ease and be content with the way things are. Staying in the valley cost less, so you think. Taking mountains cost. It requires more time, and energy along with incurring pain. It calls for you to release your untapped potential. It calls for creativity at times, and you must make good things happen. In valleys, things can just happen, and usually when things just happen, it is not good for us. In the valley, you can just survive, versus living according to your compass. When you take the mountainous route, you must be purposeful about the type of life you desire to live, because **reaching the peaks in life does not happen by accident, happenstances, or luck. It happens when you are purpose driven on the path of your compass**.

I suggest the following 7Cs as it pertains to taking the Mountain versus the Valley during our Life Compass journey. I use the number seven because I believe that the number seven is the number of completion and perfection. It derives much of its meaning from being directly connected to God's creation of all things. I also believe that when they are embraced as life principles, they can help guide us on our path, and help us arrive at our True North which is our destiny. These 7Cs are also the underlining principles of this book: Clarity, Commitment, Consistency, Courage, Conviction, Confidence, and Constraints. I expound on these 7Cs in the concluding chapter – Chapter sixteen.

CLARITY – *The clearer you are about who you are, what you really want out of life, and where you are going, the more likely you will live to your fullest, achieve what you want, and eventually arrive where you want to be.*

COMMITMENT – *Be so committed to living your best life that you, sell yourself on yourself, to the point that you make an agreement and a pledge to yourself to never stop going for what you believe is yours.*

CONSISTENCY – *Keep knocking the hell out of the obstacles that stand between you and your great destiny, until you break through them. If you keep hitting something hard enough and long enough, you will eventually break through it.*

COURAGE – *Courage is not about never being afraid. It is not about never facing obstacles that seek to block you from succeeding. Courage is about looking your fears in the eye and not shrinking back. Courage is about having the tenacity to push through what stands in your way to reach the point of your success.*

CONVICTION – *A person without conviction will lay down for anything and stand up for nothing. You must have conviction to live your best life. Without conviction the path you take will be guided by the opinion of others and by what is deemed to be most popular.*

CONFIDENCE – *It is not what others believe about you that raises you to your next level. Neither is it about what others do not believe about you that pulls you down to lower levels. What raises you to your next level or pulls you down to lower levels is the confidence you have in yourself.*

CONSTRAINTS – *Life cannot be lived at its best without limits and discipline. Without constraints one will say yes to the wrong things and no to the right things. A person without constraints is like a balloon filled with helium and let go in the wind. They will end up anywhere.*

Keeping Balance

Maintaining your balance as you follow your compass is important if you are to stay on your truest path because life presents various episodes that tend to throw you off balance. Life can present one balancing act after another. Attempting to keep your balance as you follow your life should be a priority if you expect your life to yield its best fruit as you live according to your compass. There are several things you can do that will help you keep your balance.

To maintain balance, you should keep your mind and heart focused on your purpose for being alive. You should not give your attention to the things that draw your attention from our purpose.

To maintain balance, you should embrace discipline as a major ingredient for your stability. Without discipline, you give yourself to things that do not help you in becoming all you can become. When you live beneath who you are created to be, your life gets off balance.

To maintain balance, you should be true to yourself as much as possible. By acknowledging who you are, as well as your weaknesses and strength, you are equipped to combat the temptations and fears that sometimes throw you off balance.

To maintain balance, keeping the faith is a major key to stability. You should keep in mind that Creator is for you and that all things are possible even when you are walking a tight rope in the wind.

Stick with the Process!

To keep your balance as you follow the path of your Life Compass it is imperative that you stick with the process as you move closer to your True North. Everything and everybody that progresses goes through some type of process.

Reaching any goal in life requires a process and sticking with it. Living according to your Life Compass is not simply a mindset. It is also a goal to be carried out and accomplished each day you're awake. Like any goal, for it to be accomplished you must stick with the process. Living according to your compass is a continual process. You must stick with the process of compassing if you are going to see your dreams become reality, as well as reach your destiny as you follow the path of your compass.

According to the average definition of process, it alludes to a series of actions directed to some end. It is continuous actions, operations or series of changes that take place in a definite manner towards a certain end.

When I was a boy growing up in the hood in Dallas Texas, I loved going with my friends to buy "Corn Suckers" from the Candy Lady who lived up the street and sold candy and other snacks out of her house. For those who have no clue of what a real "Corn Sucker" is, let me explain it to you. The "Corn Sucker" was candy on a stick that was made to resemble corn on a cob. The "Corn Sucker" was really a "Coin Sucker." What really made the "Corn Sucker" a "Coin Sucker" was the coin that was in the candy. In the candy, there would be a penny, a nickel, or a dime. If it were a good day, you would get a sucker with a quarter in it.

You would not know what amount of coin you had in the sucker until you went through the process of licking the candy from around the coin. This was a long, but tasteful process.

One day, some friends and I decided that we were not going to spend our time going through the process of licking the candy to get to the coin. We decided to get hammers and break the candy from around the coin. To our surprise, the candy was made up of ingredients that prevented one from getting to the coin without going through the process of licking the candy from around the coin to get to it.

Developing a life that is compass driven and maintaining the path of your compass is a process. Living compass driven is about directing your energy, time, and actions towards getting to your True North that is your destiny. It is about embracing the necessary changes that are needed to get you to the place you have pictured being as you follow the path of your compass.

Living a compass driven life is not always an easy task, because you will be tempted at times to either try to bypass the process or speed the process up. Everything that has life must go through its full term for it to grow and be healthy. When you bypass or speed up the process that is involved in living compass driven, you miss some of the vital lessons needed that drives you closer to where you are created to be. Therefore, you run the risk of missing some of the great opportunities that being compass driven provides.

Life never pans out the way it is intended to, dreams seldom become reality, and goals are not accomplished when we do not stick with the process. Again, sticking with the process of your compass is not an easy thing to accomplish for there are many things that would draw your attention, energy, and time from working out the process.

I offer the following as it relates to sticking with the process of our compass that brings dreams and goals to their manifestations:

Watch your time: If you are going to stick with the process of our compass, watching how you use your time is important. Process includes timing. Everything in life has a time. If you do not practice being a watcher of time, you will waste it on trivial matters while being stuck in meaningless moments.

Guard yourself against meaningless distractions: One of the enemies of progression is distractions. One must make up in their minds that everything cannot be important. When it comes to sticking with the process, you must determine what stays and who stays.

Keep your faith focused: Faith is vital to sticking with the process because you will not always see immediate fruit that comes from your labor. Without faith, you can easily give up on what you believe will come to be reality based upon hard work.

Guard yourself against procrastination: Procrastination stops you in the process. Process is a verb, and it bespeaks of movement and action that is exerted in a certain direction, towards a certain thing, with a certain result in mind. Procrastination keeps you in a dream state, and not working on the dream.

Value Solitude: If you are going to stick with the process of your compass, you must condition yourself for solitude. You cannot work the process always being in public view. Without solitude, you can be drawn away from the table of work, learning and planning the steps in the process.

Chapter 2

Finding Your True North

"A committed champion is one who will do what it takes for as long as it takes to fulfill, manifest and live their God-given destiny."

-John Di Lemme

A compass has an "N" sign which signifies true North latitude. North never changes regardless of the direction we go. If we were walking in the woods with a compass or driving down a highway while using a navigational system and decided to go South, East, or West, the North will never stop being North. North is always true. It was created this way. The universe and the world are created with a North that never changes regardless of what happens in the universe or the world. The universe and the world experience various changes, some good, and others not so good. But whatever has occurred, North has remained true. It cannot be changed. It is an intricate part of nature, and it remains true to the purpose for which it has been created. If we would get lost in the woods or on a highway or in the city or country, if we decided to go North, we could do so, because it will never change. It will always be true.

Every person born into this world despite their beginning, culture, gender, or family lineage, has been created with what I call a "True North." __Our True North can be defined as the arrival point in our journey for which we have been born that gives us a sense of fulfillment. It is that place that makes us feel connected with the power of creation that empowers us to use our full potential and enjoy doing it. It is the place where we are supposed to be. It is our destiny.__ It is that place where everything in creation is supposed to be by its nature. We are created with it and created for it and given the abilities to arrive at it. Your True North is that place you arrive and do the awesome things you are gifted to do naturally with passion, commitment, and contentment that impact your life and the lives of others.

How to Find Your True North

You will never find your True North until you look within yourself. Your True North is something that is within you. You are born with it, even though it takes time to discover it. You will not discover your True North by searching the world first. You find it by self-discovery and through self-acknowledgement. To find your True North you must be daring enough to go deep within yourself and discover who you are and admit what you genuinely enjoy doing and want to do.

Finding your True North is not necessarily about you accumulating more material possessions, or the accumulation of monetary wealth, even though nothing is wrong with having nice things or being wealthy. Finding your True North and living accordingly is about finally arriving at that place in your life where you can finally begin living your best life that is not dependent upon outside props.

Even if you long to arrive at a certain place in your life, you do not arrive there simply because you think about it, wish for it, or even pray about it. Some people assume that if they continue to think about arriving at a certain place in their life, wish for it hard enough, and pray about it they will eventually arrive at that place. If you want to arrive at a particular place in your life, you must accompany your thinking, wishes, and prayers concerning that place with actions that lead you down the path of your compass that will eventually get you to that place. No one arrives at a place without first putting forth action.

As you begin to live a compass driven life that will eventually lead to your True North, you must ask yourself the question, "Am I on the right path that leads to my destiny, if so, what are the indicators that I'm on the path or off the path?

There are indicators that inform you that you are on the right path leading to your True North. Here are ten of them:

You concentrate more on the present and the future than you do your past: When you are on the path that is leading to your True North you tend to be determined to focus on the possibilities that exist in your present and are excited about the possibilities of your future, even though the pain and disappointments of your past tend to creep in occasionally, but you do not entertain them to the point that they affect you.

Your inner crowd begins to thin out: When you make the decision to focus more on the path that leads to your True North it does not go unnoticed by those closest to you. It shows in your demeanor, how you talk and what you talk about. You tend to be less interested in what interested you before because you have entered a new season of life. Some of the people in your inner crowd may become uncomfortable with the changes you are making and begin to detach themselves from you. These detachments are not necessarily malicious, they are just natural.

You are more excited about waking up each day: Even when you are physically or mentally exhausted from the work you have put in the previous day, you tend to still be excited when you wake up each morning because you know that there are meaningful tasks ahead that will allow you to live and act within your purpose that you know will eventually get you to your True North.

You do not turn off your imagination about your future: When you are on the path that will eventually lead to your True North, your imagination tends to flow naturally towards what you envision your life becoming in the future. You tend to daydream about new possibilities.

You feel a sense of peace about the path you have chosen: No one's life is without struggles. We all have the tendency to feel stressed, nervous, anxious, unhappy, and exhausted from time to time. It is a part of the human equation. However, when it comes to you knowing if you are on the path that leads to your True North, one of the indicators that you have chosen the right path is you, feeling a sense of peace about the path you have chosen despite the stress, nervousness, anxiety, unhappy feelings, and exhaustion. The sense of peace comes from you knowing that you are going in the right direction.

You spend less time giving your attention to trivial things: Entertaining trivial things can cause you to waste valuable time and energy while failing to give time and energy to the things that really matters. People who are on their right path usually do not like wasting time and energy on things that do not have meaning or add positively to them while they are on their journey to their True North. Even when they are on vacation or participating in recreation or engaged in a hobby they do so while keeping their path in mind because they understand that these types of activities are part of their self-care as they continue their journey towards their True North.

You are not living passively: People who are engaged in living according to the path that leads to their True North make things happen, rather than waiting for something to happen. They are responsible for the life they live. They do not live their lives on automatic pilot. They are determined to go in a certain direction because they understand that living their best life does not happen because they get out of bed each morning, but it happens because they make it their business to make it happen.

You do not spend your time comparing yourself to others: People who are busy following the path that leads to their True North do not spend their time and energy measuring themselves to others, because they are more secure within themselves and understand that everyone is unique in their own way. Instead of comparing themselves to others, they learn from others because they understand that everyone has something unique to offer to the world.

You feel unsettled: Feeling unsettled at times is not necessarily bad. Feeling unsettled may be an indication that you realize that there is more in you that you have not released into the world. You realize that you have more to give. When you are on the path that is leading to your True North, you tend to refuse to settle for where you are in life even if you are in a good place. You press your life to the maximum.

You care less than usual about what other people think about you: We are social creatures by nature, and we care about how others perceive us. However, when your life is in alignment with the path that leads to your True North, you tend to be less concerned about getting the approval of other people for the path you have chosen. You do not need confirmation from others concerning the path you have chosen because you feel confident and good about the great possibilities you see ahead of you.

As there are indicators that inform you that you are on the right path that leads to your True North, there are also indicators that inform you that you are not on the right path or have gotten off the path that leads to your True North. Here are ten of them:

You have no sense of your purpose, or you have lost your sense of purpose: You are born with a purpose. No one is born into this world to simply exist. You are born into this world to accomplish something that only you can accomplish. Knowing your purpose and living according to it helps you down the path that will eventually get you to your True North. When you have no sense of what your purpose is in life is, you have lost your sense of purpose it is a sign that you are not on your path, or have gotten off the path that leads to your True North. When this is evident, you must make it your business to identify your purpose and become determined to get in accordance with your purpose.

You tend to live by automatic pilot versus by intentionality: There are some things in life that are out of our control. However, choosing the direction your life goes is not one of them. You have the power to choose the direction your life goes. You should never live by accident, or by happenstance if you are going to get to your True North. When you live your life by automatic pilot your life can go in any direction it chooses to. Usually, you do not arrive at the place where you can fulfill your purpose. If you are going to reach your True North, you must take your life off automatic pilot and begin to be intentional about the direction your life goes.

You focus on your past more than you do your present and your future: One of the signs that you are not on the path or have gotten off the path that leads to your True North is being more focused on your past rather than focusing on the possibilities of your present or the future. When you focus more on your past than you do your present and future, you will find yourself going backwards instead of forwards and duplicating similar events that have occurred in your previous life. This is never the right thing to do if you plan to arrive at your True North. When you realize that you are focusing more on your past more than you are on the future, you must be deliberate in changing your focus on the present and future possibilities.

You are not excited about waking up each day: When you are not on the path or have gotten off the path that leads to your True North, you are not usually excited when the alarm clock goes off because you dread the fact that you will be engaging in tasks that do not excite you or you have lost the enthusiasm about. This tends to happen because you are not challenged to use your talents, potential, abilities, and giftedness. When this is the case, it becomes important that you strongly consider making vital changes in your life, even if it means considering changing careers or locations, or even changing your perspective on what you do daily.

You can be easily attracted to trivial things: When you are not on the path or have gotten off the path that leads to your True North, you tend to be easily attracted to trivial things. As a result, you get caught-up in the cycle of giving a great amount of your time and energy to things and even people that do not add value to you or do not help you fulfill your purpose. To break this cycle, you must be disciplined enough to say "No" to things that do not add meaning to you, even if they mean something to others.

You do not envision a great future: When you are on the right path that is leading to your True North, you envision better days ahead despite your present condition of existence. On the other hand, when you are not on the right path or have gotten off the path, you can become blinded from the great future that is in front of you. When this is the case, you either live your life according to your past, or your life comes to a standstill, and you fail to do the things you need to do to embrace your destiny. If you are going to envision a great future, you must resurge your enthusiasm about living your best life possible.

You feel no sense of peace: We all experience disturbing situations from time to time. When you are on the right path that leads to your True North, you have a sense of peace regardless of unpleasant situations, because you know that you will eventually get to a place where you can fulfill your purpose, and you envision a better life that awaits you down the path. On the other hand, when you are not on that path or have ventured off the path for one reason or another, you sometimes have nothing positive to look forward to that will add peace to your life. The best thing to do at this point is to make up your mind that you will do your best to get on the right path and stay on it.

You settle for things as they are: One of the indicators that we are not on the right path or have gotten off the right path that is going in the direction of our True North is settling for things as they are without putting forth a real effort to change them for the better. When you settle for a thing as they are instead of pressing your life to its maximum even though you know that life has more to offer and that you have the potential to do more and accomplish more, you live at your minimum. When this is the case, to get on the right path and maintain your momentum, you must refuse to stay stuck and minimum and begin pressing yourself to the maximum.

You are caught-up in the trap of Comparison: Comparison is a trap that can go undetected and can easily keep you from getting on the path or can easily draw you off the path that leads to your True North. This is because while you are busy comparing yourself to others, you fail to appreciate and celebrate yourself. Because you devalue who you are, as well as the positive contribution you can make to the world. You will never get on the right path or stay on the path that leads to your True North if you believe that someone else's grass is always greener than yours while failing to cultivate your grass to make it greener. To get on the right path or to get back on the right path, you must value who you are and your potential, as well as what you have to offer others as you live according to your purpose.

You are overly concerned about what others think about you: One of the signs that you are not on the path or have gotten off the path that leads to your True North is, aligning your life according to the perception of others. You need the approval of other people concerning the path you choose. You become people pleasers to the extent that you attempt to live according to the path that others say you should be on, versus choosing your own path. Only you know the real path that you should be taking. Others are recipients of the path you take and not the makers of your path. When you believe that others know what is best for you than you do yourself, you will pattern your life according to their pleasure. The only way you can break free of being overly concerned about what others think about you and about the path you are taking is to finally get to a point where you are all right with yourself regardless of your flaw. Being overly concerned about what other people think about you can become an unnecessary weight to carry and can prevent you from reaching your True North.

How to Know You are at Your True North

We can know when we have arrived at our True North. Arriving at your True North is about being and living within your essence in which you embrace what really brings you joy, peace, self-love, self-esteem, harmony, and the true love you express to others.

You will know when you have arrived at your True North when you begin waking up each morning excited about what you will be doing during the day. You have arrived at your True North when you wake up in the morning and do what you do with passion, even if you did not make a check. It is waking up each morning and doing what you love doing most. Steve Harvey said, "If the alarm clock goes off in the morning, and you don't want to get out of bed, you are not doing what you're supposed to be doing." When You arrive at your True North, you are usually excited when the clock goes off, because you get to do what you love doing and are created to do.

Every person has a True North even if it is not recognized or acknowledged. True North is about what you are created for and equipped to do with less strain. Operating according to your True North is simply doing what you are created to do and being successful at it. It also suggests that anything that is alive has a True North, whether it is family, personal life, marriage, business, etc. If something or someone is to reach their destiny and be successful at performing it, they must embrace its True North.

Notice the animal world. Tigers and lions function differently in the wild even though they are of the cat family. This is because even though they are of the same species, they are wired differently to function differently in the wild. For example, they hunt differently. Tigers hunt for food in the jungle on their own during the night and eat their catch alone, whereas lions leave the hunting job to the female lion, who carries out the hunt in groups and bring their prey to the pride. Therefore, one can deduce that lions are more sociable, and tigers are more solitary. They seem to know their True North – that for which they are created to perform which allows them to live successfully in the wild.

I have discovered in my own life experiences, as well as my conversations with others, that even though we are born with a True North, it is not easily discovered and lived out. This is because as kids and youth, we were often impressed upon by our parents or by society to be someone or something that did not match our natural uniqueness. Whenever we fail at embracing our uniqueness, we fail at reaching and living out our destiny. We were seldom taught to be true to ourselves, but to emulate others, or attempt to do something that we were not born or gifted to do. Such teaching is usually handed down generationally and is usually based upon how we were taught by our parents and societal norms.

Even though discovering our True North and living accordingly is not an easy task, it can be embraced and lived out. It is a matter of choice that may require some help and direction. It also requires that we do a self-inventory and be true to ourselves and discover our own God given uniqueness. We are all unique and should embrace it and not be ashamed of it. This should be done without apology.

Own Who You Are

<u>**One of the most important things you can ever do is to own who you are**</u>. Life compassing is about taking your true path seriously to lead you to your True North. That place and position in life where you live with passion and feel complete without needing permission from others to do so. I have discovered that finding and arriving at your True North is not easy, because we have various preexisting things in our lives that get in the way. One of the obstacles that often gets in the way of reaching your True North is not owning who you are. I mean the good you, the strong you, the person who loves and cares for others, the gifted you. Some people are not stuck in life where they are because they are not good, strong, loving, and caring or not gifted. Some people are stuck where they are in life because they fail to own up to who they are and who they have been created to be. As a matter of fact, you will never live according to your Life Compass if you never come to grips with who you are and who you are created to be. When you do not own up to who you are and who you are created to be, you will take paths that do not fit you. This is sometimes due to ascertaining that someone else's path is better than your own. You should be careful to not long for

the path of others because you do not know the price they have paid or paying for the path they are on. The wisest and most rewarding thing you can do is stay on your own path. When you stay on your path, you will arrive at your destiny.

Again, when I talk about owning who you are, I am speaking about finally coming to a place in your compassed journey where you finally grasp the good, strong, loving, caring, gifted you, who has gotten lost in the hustle and the bustle of life, or the one who has spent more time being an impressionist versus authentic.

Owning who we are can be a task within itself because society presses upon you to live a manufactured life. You are not encouraged often to be authentic. You are encouraged to duplicate and to fit in.

Owning who you are is intentional. It does not happen by accident or by happenstance. It is not a one-time thing. To live the life, you are created and gifted to live, you must embrace owning who you are as a lifestyle.

Self-Admission

To embrace and own who you are, you must arrive at a place of Self-Admission. When it comes to living according to your Life Compass and reaching our True North, it is imperative that we engage in self-admission. **Self-admission is an acknowledgement of the truth about self.** Self-admission can be hard to do as well as scary at times. This depends on your perspective. Even though self-admission unveils your weaknesses, they can sometimes be overcome as you embrace your true strengths. It is not always about fixing what is broken versus it being about nurturing our strengths that override our weaknesses. Self-admission does not have to be hard or scary. It does not have to be negative,

34

because all your truth is not negative. Self-admission can be freeing, empowering, refreshing, and confirming. Self-admission helps in several ways.

Self-admission helps you identify the areas of our true giftedness. Everyone is born with their own unique gifts and should own their giftedness and use it as much as possible to stay the path that leads to your destiny.

Self-admission helps identify what makes you happy. When you admit to what makes you happy, less time is wasted entertaining the things or people who make you sad.

Self-admission helps you identify what type of life you desire to live. If you do not know what type of life you want to live, your life ends up resembling something you do not want.

Self-admission helps you identify the truth of who you are presently while helping you grasp who you can become. When you admit to the truth of who you are authentically, you discover that you are not totally bad. You discover that you are a wonderful unique creation of the Creator.

Self-admission helps you to identify what drives you. Drives can be defined as those things that set you off in a particular direction. All these drives are not negative, neither are all the directions you are driven are negative. Drivers can be positive because they take you down the path of your truest passion.

Taking Charge

It is time to admit to your goodness, uniqueness, and your beautiful truth that will empower you to live the life you are capable of living. This calls for taking charge.

You will never do what you are empowered to do, and your life will never produce what it can, neither will you go in the direction you dream of going until you take charge of the life you are gifted. You have been granted the power and the possibilities to change things in your life. Regardless of where you have been or where you are in life presently – regardless of your misfortunes, mistakes, or bad decisions, each day you awake and take the challenge of getting out of bed and deciding to take the advantage of the new day you are given, you have the chance to change things if you resolve to take charge. So, take charge of your life and stop letting the circumstances that take place or have taken place in your life have charge over you.

Many of the changes that take place in your life that empowers and makes a positive difference in your life are not necessarily the immediate changing of your circumstances or the changes that take place in the lives of those around you, but it is found in the change that takes place in you once you resolve to take charge of your own life and determine what type of life you really want to live, as well as the direction you want your life to go.

Instead of living your life by accident, luck, or happenstance, you must decide to take charge of the course that your life goes and live it purposefully. To live according to your Life Compass and arrive at your destiny, you must take charge and become the creative painter and begin painting the picture of what you envision your life becoming on the blank life canvas you have been given regardless of its size, and no matter if you do not presently have the resources needed. When you honestly resolve to take charge of painting the picture of the direction your life goes, you will discover various ways to make it a reality.

When I was in high school, I was afforded the opportunity to study art at SMU Meadows School of the Arts in Dallas. Because my mother could not afford to buy me the paint brushes, I needed, I would go through the trash and retrieve the paint bushes that other students would throw away at the end of each semester, because I had honestly resolved that I wanted to learn how to paint by any means necessary. When we honestly take charge and make the honest decision that we are going to paint a new picture of our life even if we do not have the immediate resources or must paint over the picture that has already been painted for us, the universe has a way of giving us what we need. But it will only afford us what we need when we begin taking charge and choosing the direction we go.

Choosing Your Direction

Bob Marley said, "Every man gotta right to decide his own destiny." We decide our own destiny when we choose our own direction. **There are some things in life we cannot control, but the direction our life goes is not one of them.** We have been equipped with whatever we need to aim our lives in a certain direction. This needs no approval of others. The direction in which we go is a matter of choice and not by happenstance, neither is it determined by the various negative events we encounter. Those who arrive at their destiny are those who are determined to choose the direction they go despite their negative encounters.

The direction you go in life is an individual choice, and you must be the one to choose it. If you do not take control of the direction you go, life will go according to the flow of your circumstances and situations. A life without deliberate direction is like sand caught in a high wind which moves in the direction the wind takes it. You should not live like the sand on a beach that is moved by the winds. When it comes to sticking to the direction you have chosen, you should be like heavy stones embedded in the earth that are not easily moved by life winds.

You cannot control what life brings or issues out, but you can control the direction you allow it to take you. You control the direction your life goes when you try your hardest to go according to your God given potential and essence. This is not always an easy task to accomplish, but it can be accomplished. Life changes according to the direction you choose and the direction you choose changes your life.

Chapter 3
Your Magnetic Pull

"Even when you think you have life all mapped out, things happen that shape your destiny in ways you might never have imagined."

-Deepak Chopra

As referred to earlier in the book, a compass is a tool for finding direction. It has a magnetic needle mounted on a pivot or short pin. The needle can spin freely and will always point to True North. If you have ever been hiking, you probably used a compass to help you stay on your path that leads to your destination. You noticed that the needle in the compass responds to the planet's magnetism.

The compass needle aligns itself and points towards the top of the Earth's magnetic field, giving explorers and lost souls a consistent sense of direction that allows them to arrive at their appointed destination. The needle in the compass is drawn by what is called "magnetism." Magnetism is simply defined as a physical phenomenon produced by the motion of electric charges resulting in attractions and repulsive forces between objects. Magnetism in our daily lives is a magnetic invisible pull that we sometimes respond to without noticing it. Have you ever wondered why you are drawn to some things, certain thoughts, feelings about something, dreams, and visions that seem to be hard to shake? Well, this is magnetism. These feelings and desires are what I call "Magnetic Pull."

Each of us is born with a natural compass that contains a magnetic pull. The purpose of this magnetic pull is to draw you in the direction of our True North. I defined earlier, that your True North is the destiny for which you have been created to arrive at that makes life more enjoyable. The fact is each of us has a destiny and it is what makes life work. The only way we can arrive at that place of destiny where life becomes more empowering and enjoyable, it is imperative that we pay attention to our magnetic pull and embrace it and move accordingly.

Unfortunately, many people go through life never recognizing or embracing their Magnetic Pull. This is sometimes due to being lured to things or careers others may believe is a good fit for you, even when you know differently. In addition, sometimes failing at embracing your Magnetic Pull and moving accordingly, you sometimes reject the fact that you have outgrown some things, certain careers, and even certain people, that once made you feel fulfilled. When this is the case, you go in directions and take paths that do not coincide with your Life Compass. **<u>Your Magnetic Pull can be defined as those sensations that drives and pull you closer to the destination for which you are created and can reach</u>**.

Your Magnetic Pull happens at the core of your being. It has more to do with what is in you and what you have been born for, versus what is on the surface of your being. There is more to you than meets the eye. The things that drive and pull you in certain directions in life happens at your core. When you are constantly being pulled towards certain directions, then decide to ignore the pull, and go opposite the direction you are being driven to or resolve to remain where you in life, your Magnetic Pull tugs at you from the inside out, versus the outside in. Your core is connected to our Creator who created us with positive purpose and desires, and if they are acknowledged, and embraced, they can lead to the path of your compass, and you will eventually reach your destiny. Living your life according to your Magnetic Pull being connected to your core is a process.

Let me explain how this process works. First, acknowledge and accept the Creator, who I acknowledge as God, at the core of my existence. God is our source of energy and life. God only desires the best for His creation, even if what and who He has created ignore Him or not. In John 10:10 Jesus says, that, *"He has come that we have life to the full."* This means that God has created us to live full lives. Therefore, because God desires for us to live full lives, He constantly pulls at our core to lead us to the destiny for which we are created, by infusing us with certain desires, passions, and instincts by which our lives become clearer, and we discover what we really want. Secondly, when we acknowledge and accept the fact that God is our Creator and desires the best for us, we become partners with Him as we recreate and redefine ourselves according to our Life Compass. However, when we ignore the Creator's pull at our core, we find ourselves living from the outside in, instead of the inside out. Which draws us off our compass and we delay arriving at our True North which is our God given destiny.

Living Inside Out

To get the most and the best out of life starts from the inside. Before I explain the meaning of living inside out, let me explain what I contend living outside in means. To me living outside in means to pattern our lives based upon events that take place around us, and affects how we view the world around us, as well as what one may call societal norms. Societal norms can be defined as practices and beliefs that society says are the only way life can be lived at its best. There are times when societal norms overlook or do not take into consideration individuality. This is not to say that societal norms do not play a role in our lives. However, it is to say that while amid societal norms, we should be careful not to ignore or bypass our individual desires, passions, and instincts that are at the core of our existence as we are connected to the Creator.

When we resolve to live life, solely dictated by the events that occur around us as well as by societal norms without keeping in mind our core desires, passions, and instincts, we get off course of our Life Compass and we take paths for the sake of satisfying others and perhaps to maintain some type of popularity, which sometimes causes us to lose sight of who we are created to be and the life we deeply desire to live. This can sometimes make for a miserable life.

I must admit that prior to arriving at a point in my life where I began rediscovering more of myself, as well as attempting to redefine myself and acknowledging what I really want the rest of my life, as I embrace my core – my desires, passions, and instincts, my life was somewhat miserable, even though some persons who knew me considered me as successful. People did not understand that there was more going on underneath the surface of my existence. I was being pulled by my Magnetic Pull that was connected to my core and the Creator who desire for me to live my best life. This became uncomfortable to me because I was being pulled outside of my comfort zones and away from some things and some ways of doing things to which I had become accustomed and entrenched in. The majority of what I thought was happiness was more connected to how well things were going on around me, versus how well I was feeling on the inside. I allowed the things and people outside of my core existence to lead me down a path that I knew was not in concert with the shift of my season that I deeply knew that the Creator was taking me. It was not until I began reading the book written by Dr. Frank A. Thomas, Professor of Homiletics at Christian Theological Seminary, entitled "*The Choice*," that I came to grips with the reality that for several years, I had been living my life from the outside in versus living from the inside out. Most of what I was starting to do was based upon what people believed I should be about for their mere satisfaction and approval. Dr. Thomas says, "...we must come to acknowledge Jesus Christ at the inner core of our being. In this acceptance at our inner core, we come to know what we believe to be true. Only when we know what is true do we come to know what we want, really. Upon discovering what we want, really, our passion becomes clear to us. Once our passion is clear, it helps us to locate a deep need in the exterior world, and we discover the joy of a vocation, or what many know as a "call." Upon the discovery of this vocational call, we partner with God and discover work for our head, heart, hands, and feet to do. In doing this work, we discover that we must re-engineer or re-create our entire lives, or we must do our creative best to reshape our entire lives to live the vocational call." The vocational call is not simply about the career we choose. It can also be defined as a strong impulse and inclination to function in a particular station in life that comes from beyond oneself. In a nutshell, it is our Magnetic Pull that comes from beyond oneself that puts us on the path according to our Life Compass, that gets us to our True North.

Your Calling

What are you really called to do? What do you really want to be doing in your life currently? Are you doing what you want to do or are you just doing what you do to make ends meet? Believe me, I totally understand. Sometimes we lose our truest calling in the hustle and bustle of making a living – raising children, paying bills trying to make ends meet while trying to prove to others that we are alright and that we deserve their love and attention. I have been there and done that until I arrived at a place where I wanted to see myself again, as well as know what I was really called to do the rest of my life.

As far as I can remember, I always thought that "calling," was only related to those who were called into the preaching ministry. I was called into the preaching ministry at the age of eighteen when I was a junior in high school. That was as far as calling went for me. At that time, I did not know that other people who were not called to preach the gospel had a calling on their life. It was not until I woke up one morning and realized that what I was once called to do as a pastor was no longer in me. What a disturbance! All I knew was pastoring congregations. God revealed to me that He had given me more abilities that I had not been using because I had not paid attention to my Magnetic Pull. I concluded that I was caught up in something that I knew was a calling on my life, but was beginning to cause me to feel stagnant because I was not exploring other options and levels of my calling in a deeper way. I discovered that our calling has various levels that are sometimes not acknowledged. It is like a house with different rooms, but the same house. What we are truly called to do never changes because it is connected to our destiny. However, the levels of our calling changes, depending on the season in which our compass leads us. This sometimes calls for us to be open to the shifts of our seasons. **Because your seasons shift does not mean your calling has changed**. It simply means that we begin to explore innovative ways to carry out our truest calling. I conclude that there are others who are facing similar dilemmas. So, I present this book as a way of informing others that even if you have a career or embraced a particular calling on your life presently or formerly, there is more that awaits you. Each of us has a calling on our lives no matter what our present station is in life. The question is, are you willing to adhere to the next level of your calling or next calling? I came to realize that even though I had lived my life according to a particular calling on my life and had done well according to those who was on the outside looking in, the Creator was shifting my season in which I would be challenged to embrace the next level of my calling. This would take me having the courage and faith to shift with my season which is both challenging and scary, because of the unknown. Our calling can be described as that tug and pull, passion, drive, and sensation that we wake up with every morning that drives us through the day, as well as into the next season of our lives. This calling is connected to our Life Compass, which leads us to our Truest North which is our destiny, and guided by our Magnetic pull, which is the Creator who desires the best for us. To embrace our calling, we must acknowledge and embrace our passions.

Embracing Your Passion

Passion can be described as your true self as it relates to the things that drives us. It is about doing the things that make us the happiest, that we are most proud of and enthusiastic about, and leaves us feeling fulfilled. To live according to your Life Compass, it is imperative that we make an honest attempt to identify and acknowledge our truest passions. When we embrace and acknowledge our truest passion we will eventually arrive at our Truest North. For this to become a reality, we must ask ourselves, what is it that drives us through life? Are we living by happenstance and luck, hoping that our lives will eventually resemble the picture we have painted? The truth of the matter of life is that our lives will never resemble or come close to resembling the picture we have painted until we begin approaching each day with passion. To become good at something and master it, we must be passionate about it. So, it is with living life. If we want the best out of life as we live according to our compass, we must approach life with passion, that powerful compelling emotion or deep arousal. Here are several ways we can embrace our passion.

Be open minded to try something that you have been wanting to try but never have. Living with passion calls for trying something new.

Be curious about what else life has to offer. Our passion reveals new things.

Be spontaneous and do not always play by the rules. Passion drives us beyond the average.

Be brave enough to color outside the lines of your life. Your life is your personal coloring book. Passion brings out your creativity.

Be enthusiastic about living life at its best. Passion causes us to get excited each day looking for the best no matter what.

Be willing to live your life out loud and in the open. Do not settle for being a zero or invisible to the world. Let the world see and hear your passion for life.

Be courageous and take a risk. If we want something bad enough, we must be willing to pay the cost. Living life passionately is not without a price, but it pays off in the long run.

Be daring to have fun with the life you have. Let your inner child run free on the playground of your life. Living life passionately adds fun to life.

Restoring Your Soul

To be sensitive to your Magnetic Pull and live from your inner core, adhere to your calling, and embrace your passion while making an honest effort to follow your compass, you should practice restoring your soul on a regular basis. Restoring your soul is important if you are to follow the path of your compass and reach your destiny. The soul is defined as the principle of life, feelings, thoughts, and actions in humans, regarded as a distinct entity separate from the body. It is considered as the spiritual part of your existence. As it is important for us to restore our bodies, it is just as important to restore our souls regularly.

Several years ago, prior to arriving at the point where I began thinking seriously about living my life according to my Life Compass, I discovered that my soul needed to be restored even though I had what I believed was a close connection with the Creator who was pulling me closer to my destiny. I thought that because I was heavily involved in Christendom, the soul part of me was alright. But something was missing. I discovered that even though I was heavily involved in Christendom, I did not make much time to restore my soul. As a result, I was spending most of my time attempting to make sure that the outer me resembled a perfect picture that society had painted as a picture of success and a happy person. But underneath the surface of my existence, I was not living according to my compass because the inner me – my soul was running on empty and needed to be restored. The more my soul needed to be restored the more deemed my truest destiny became. Once I discovered this need, I started the journey of practicing restoring my soul. I hope that you will strongly consider the same as you follow your Life Compass as you are being pulled to your truest destiny.

Our soul is the seat of our existence, it is the basis of our principles, feeling, thoughts, emotions, and actions. Our soul is our inner Sanctum. When our soul needs restoration, our inner sanctum is thrown off balance. This calls for soul restoration. Restoring is to bring something back into existence, or back into its original or normal condition. To restore our soul, we must be intentional about being in connection with God who is our ultimate source for restoration, and desires to restore our souls, Psalm 23:1-3 (NIV), *"The Lord is my shepherd, I lack nothing. He makes me lie down in green pastures, he leads me besides quiet waters, he refreshes my soul. He guides me along the right paths for his name's sake."* Our soul can be restored when we consider practices what I call the 4Rs for Soul Restoration—*Recess, Relax, Reflect* and *Readjust*:

Recess: When we recess, we temporally withdraw from our routine. When I was in elementary school, we would have recess. Recess was that time that was allowed for students to break away from the studies that we were engaged in during the early part of the day. It also gave us a chance to play as we regrouped for the remainder of the day. Unfortunately, as we became adults, we somehow lost the art of recessing. There are times when we need to get out of the hustle and the race for our soul to rest and be restored and find some time to play.

Relax: To relax is to simply chill. Many times, our lives become tightened with programs, schedules, anxiety, stress, and worries, and we forget to live life. These things tend to wear down our souls.

Therefore, it becomes important for us to make and take the time to be still and release the toxins we have accumulated over time.

Reflect: Reflection helps us to project joyful images and experiences on the walls of our mind that can restore the power of our soul. No matter your current circumstances, we all have some pleasant event that we can reflect on that can bring us joy in some sense or another. Sometimes, we may have to dig for them.

Readjust: Readjusting is about going through a process of rearranging ourselves and things in our lives that promote balance, and soul rest. We cannot restore our soul without readjusting our thoughts, emotions, habits, and routines. We must remember that the Creator will only restore our souls as we attempt to restore our own souls.

Chapter 4
Intentional Changes

*In the search for your destiny, you will often find yourself
obliged to change directions."*

-Paulo Coelho

I f we want something different, we must be willing and intentional about changing some of the things we are accustomed to doing. We change the course of our game when we change how we play in the game.

As it comes to change, the song entitled, "Everything Must Change," comes to mind which says, "Everything must change, nothing stays the same. Everyone must change, nothing stays the same... Cause that's the way of time, nothing and no one goes unchanged." The world changes, people change, we change things, and sometimes changes, change us. **For life to produce its best, we must be willing to accept change whether we like it or not. Change is a necessary ingredient in life, particularly when it comes to living our lives according to our Life Compass and staying the path that leads to our True North as we are connected to our Magnetic Pull**.

There are times when it is not easy to accept change. I discovered this in my own journey while seeking to refine myself. Even though I wanted something different in my life, I also wanted to keep things the way they were, because it was what I had become accustomed to over the years. But I came to the realization that one cannot redefine themselves by accepting change and without being intentional about changing some things that no longer fit. When I became deliberate about compassing my life, I concluded that if I were going to follow the path of my Life Compass and arrive at that place in my life where I would feel the joy of being fulfilled, I had to embrace the various seasons of change, as well as make necessary changes on my own. I hope you will consider the same for your own life.

When it comes to compassing our lives, change is necessary. Change is inevitable whether we like it or not, and it is a part of the human agenda. Even though change is inevitable, those of us who aim to live life according to our Life Compass are aware of making necessary changes. We do not wait for things to change by luck, happenstance, or accident. We make the necessary changes because we see its value, and how such changes move us closer to what we are created for. Making needed changes is not just about identifying those things and even sometimes people that no longer fit. It is about breaking negative habits. Negative habits can be defined as practices that throw us off the path of our compass, and do not push us closer to our destiny, but pushes us further from it. So, we must understand that if we are going to follow our Life Compass and find our True North, we must be about making necessary changes that call for us to reset some things in our lives.

Resetting

For something to operate at its best, there are times when resetting is necessary. Following the path of our Life Compass to get to our True North, is not possible without having the willingness to engage in "Resetting." Resetting is powerful. Through the process of resetting, we rearrange and realign our lives to match the path of our compass as we move towards our destiny. Without resetting our lives from time to time, we remain off course of our compass, by which we take by-passes that may not lead to our destiny.

Every living organism must go through a process of resetting for it to grow or evolve to its fullest. A seed does not simply become a tree. It must go through the process of resetting between stages of growth and seasons. As we are inspired to reach new levels of possibilities as we follow the path of our compass, we must take into consideration the importance of resetting.

Regardless of what we are involved in, be it pleasurable or otherwise, our bodies, minds, and souls become depleted of the energy needed to keep us focused on that which is imperative for the next level or stage in our lives. There are various encounters and experiences that cause us to lose track of our path from time to time. Therefore, it is important that we practice resetting regularly. Failing to be mindful to reset from time to time, we sometimes fall into a rut and our lives get stuck into sameness, and it does not yield the fruitful possibilities that are present in the season we are in. We fail to grasp what we need to keep growing into the person we are created to become. When this occurs, we start living our lives in neutral. When we are in neutral, we do not go backwards or forward. We just remain where we are. This is not saying that we are not mobile. It simply means that our lives come to a stand-still or take a course of their own, and we can begin to meander and fail to bear the ripe fruit it is capable of bearing. This can occur even after we have discovered our compass and know what our destiny is, if we do not reset when needed.

Resetting is about adjusting or fixing ourselves or restructuring our life in a new and different way. It can also mean **reaching back and taking a hold of those things that once worked for us, but we let go of for some reason or another. Resetting is also about streamlining our lives in accordance with our Life Compass.**

When I started making an honest attempt to move according to what I believe is my Life Compass while attempting to stay focused on what I believe is my True North, I concluded that to do so, I would have to put forth a real effort to streamline my life. In life compassing, something must give. We cannot take everything or everybody on the journey. To maintain our compass path, we must identify what and who fits us and what and who we fit.

Streamlining

Streamlining our lives is important if we are going to eventually reach our destiny. It is difficult to move forward and upward while attempting to carry everything and everybody. Surely, we can make strides and reach new levels while carrying a lot. The question is, what condition will be in when we reach the place we are trying to arrive at and the level we are trying to reach while carrying extra loads? Some loads we carry on our journey are inevitable. They are just a part of life. On the other hand, some of the loads we carry throughout our lives are not necessary. Some loads can be let go of and need to be let go of if we are going to stay the path of our Life Compass and reach our True North. We cannot carry everything, and everybody while trying to be successful as we take the path of our Life Compass as we are moving towards our True North. Again, something must give. Some of the things and even some of the people we have become accustomed to, familiar and comfortable with, we must let go of. They will not be released automatically. We must make the choice to let go. This can be a painful decision to make because some of the things and people we must release are like permanent fixtures in our lives. They have been around for a long time, and we have gotten used to them, even if they are negative and heavy.

Streamlining is about altering or removing certain things in and out of our lives to be more efficient or simpler as we take the path of our Life Compass. These things can be habits, routines, toxic people, and even certain mindsets. The list can go on.

Even though streamlining our lives is one of the most difficult and painful decisions we will make in life, it is also one of the most transforming decisions we can make. It is transforming because it allows us the chance to reinvent and redefine ourselves while getting a clearer perspective of where we are presently, and where we are trying to arrive. I learned firsthand the imperativeness of streamlining as one attempts to move forward and go to new levels while taking certain paths while climbing a mountain for the first time.

In 2007 I was afforded the awesome opportunity to serve with a mission team in the Democratic Republic of the Congo for ten days, a trip I had been waiting for. I had dreamt of traveling to Africa for many years. The opportunity came over which I was excited. We arrived in the Congo late one night and stayed at an abandoned mission facility. The following two days we spent time engaging with the Congolese people while handing out Audio Bibles translated in their language, starting a medical clinic, and mixing cement to lay bricks for a school. Several days later, our mission team was scheduled to visit a small church located on the top of a mountain. This was exciting to me because I had never climbed a mountain.

The morning of our climb I just knew I was ready, and nothing was going to stop me from getting to the top. After about a fourteen-mile hike, we arrived at the foot of the mountain, and it was time to go up. I was geared up for the climb. Before we started our ascension up the mountain, we were introduced to our guides who would be leading us. I noticed that one of our guides, a very polite African gentleman was dressed in a suit, shirt, tie, and shoes as if he were going to church on a Sunday. I said to myself, "It is no way this guy is going to reach the top dressed like that." I later found out that I was totally incorrect about my assumption.

Before starting our climb, I volunteered to carry the backpack filled with water bottles and other items we may need during our journey. The first seven to eight miles upward were no problem. It was the next few miles that got to me. I found myself sweating like a racehorse and knees about to buckle. I still had my eyes on the guide who was wearing the Sunday clothes. Sunday clothes are usually clothes that are set aside for wearing to church only. I learned this when I was a boy growing up in a single parent family. Our guide was moving up the mountain as if he did not have a care in the world. He is moving with a stride and a smile on his face as he is talking about the surrounding beauty that I am too tired to enjoy.

The other guide noticed that I was having an issue climbing while carrying the backpack. He comes to me and asks can he take the backpack. With no hesitation, I gave up the load. I streamlined.

I figured out why the guide in the suit did not have much of a problem moving forward up the mountain, it was because he was not attempting to carry an extra load. Evidently, he had made the decision to streamline before he started to climb. It was evident that he understood the fact that if he was going to move forward and upward with less strain and distraction, he had to decide what he was going to wear and take with him. This is a lesson that we all can learn, which is to decide what we take with us as we attempt to follow our compass path.

After giving up the backpack, moving forward up became easier, and I was able to take in the breathtaking beauty around me, as well as make it to the top of the mountain.

The path of our compass consists of various encounters that are inevitable but can be dealt with efficiently when we practice streamlining.

Here are 7Rs that helps us streamline for Life Compassing.

Reorganize your Priorities: Our lives can consist of things that we deem as priorities. Even though they are priorities, they must be placed according to their importance, if they are going to work for our best benefit.

Reevaluate your Commitments: Over time we tend to commit to many things. We do this sometimes without knowing that we have made a commitment to them. Which sometimes end up being a part of our routine. If we are going to follow the true path of our Life Compass, we must take time to reevaluate the things we have committed to, to see if they fit where we are in our lives presently.

Release the Past: When we look back over our past, we will discover that there are some positive things that have occurred that we must never forget. However, we will discover that there are some negative things in our past that tend to affect how we move in the present and must be released if we are going to get to our True North.

Restructure to Simplify: Restructuring is not just about building up or building larger or becoming more complex. Sometimes restructuring is about simplification. It is about decluttering – getting rid of those things that are no longer needed to see our life path more clearly.

Redefine You: During the process of life compassing, it is imperative that we get a fresh perspective of ourselves. It is not enough to streamline the things in our lives without taking the time to redefine ourselves. When we begin to streamline, we must redefine ourselves accordingly. We too must change with the new things we have set out to do and accomplish.

Review Your Crowd: We all have a crowd we relate to, whether it is large or small. The crowd we relate to influences us directly and sometimes indirectly. They influence us either positively or negatively. It has been said, "we become like the closets five people we relate to." It is urgent that while we are attempting to live a compass driven life that we take time to review those in our crowd to see which ones lean on us and wear us down and which ones lift us to be our best. Which ones pulls us down and which ones push us forward.

Refocus on Your Purpose: Why are you still here on earth? Why do you keep getting out of bed each morning? What are you supposed to be doing besides making a check, paying bills, and having fun? When we streamline it helps us refocus on our purpose, because during the process of streamlining we remove those things that have clouded our viewpoint on our purpose, and we are able to see more clearly what we should be doing and capable of being successful at.

Think Big

As streamlining is important for living compass driven, adjusting our minds to think big or bigger is also important. <u>**Limited thinking produces a limited life. The bigger our thinking the greater the chance to live the big life we dream of**</u>. Resetting our lives to follow our Life Compass is impossible without changing the level of our thinking. Proverbs 23:7 (NIV) says, *"As a man thinks in his heart, so is he."* This implies that how we think and what we think about has much to do with who we become, as well as the type of life we live. This can also be applied to our Life compass. Following our compass is not just about the action we take but it is also about the level of our thinking. I contend that as we make an honest attempt to align our lives with our compass that will eventually lead us to our destiny, it becomes imperative that we elevate our thinking pattern.

To get to the high level that following our compass provides, we must raise the level of our thinking. Therefore, we must develop the habit of thinking big or bigger.

A man's limitations are only as limited as his mind. We never arrive at a place in life without our minds arriving there first. We follow the course of our thinking. If we think small, life is small. If we think big or bigger, chances are, our lives become bigger than what it is currently.

If one cannot imagine in his mind being other than where he is, he will never arrive anywhere other than where he is. The difference between those who follow their compass and those who do not is how they think, followed by actions that enhance their thinking pattern. To follow the path of your compass and arrive at your True North, you must imagine the outcome. This starts with whether you think big or small. You cannot acquire big things while following the path of your compass thinking small or limited.

People are not small, because they are created to be small, and they do not fail to accomplish big things, because they are not capable. They are small in their minds, and they adapt only to doing small stuff because they do not allow their minds to take them somewhere that is bigger and beyond where they currently exist. We sometimes acclimate to small thinking because we allow our doubts to get the best of us, even when we know we have the potential for more and to do more. If we are going to think big, we must squash our doubts.

Squash Your Doubts

When we resolve to start thinking big outside of the box of familiarity, comfortability, and tradition, we get the attention of doubt. Don't let doubt limit how big you think and what you want and expect out of life. Some people start out thinking big but end up letting doubt take residence in their minds, and they begin to think small by which they get small results.

If you do not squash your doubts, your doubts will squash you. It will squash your dreams, your vision and prohibit you from using your potential and abilities. It will also keep you from leaping from where you are, and you can miss the awesome opportunities made available to you to take hold of, the wonderful and great things that are at your fingertips and cause you to miss moving into your new frontier. Furthermore, you will never muster the faith and confidence to follow the path of your compass and reach your true destiny if you allow doubt to keep you captive.

Some people who have identified their compass path and have a solid idea of what their true destiny is, sometimes fail at living their best life, not because of a lack of potential, but because they allow their doubt to get the best of them versus them overcoming it. Doubt is an enemy and not a friend!

- *Doubt is the enemy against positive progression.*
- *Doubt is the enemy against elevation to higher levels in life.*
- *Doubt is the enemy against the potential of greatness.*
- *Doubt is the enemy of great ideas, inventions, dreams, and visions.*

Doubt causes several things if you do not subdue it, instead of taking leaps you will remain nesting (*I'll say more about leaping and nesting in chapters fourteen and fifteen*), and instead of you being compass driven, you become driven by your doubt.

Doubt causes you to live in "what has never been." Many people are missing great opportunities to rise to new elevations in their life because they allow doubt to keep them stuck in "what has never been." Just because something has not happened, does not mean it will not happen. Do not let doubt delete your possibilities.

Doubt causes you to concentrate more on your weaknesses and less on your strength. You cannot be good at everything, but you are good at something. You must overcome doubt to release and build upon what you are good at doing and gifted for.

Doubt causes you to give away opportunities that belong to you. Many people are missing awesome opportunities to live their life on new levels because they allow their doubt to talk them out of their opportunities. Doubt says things like, "You do not have enough money to reach your dream – you do not have enough support to get the job done – you are too young or too old and no one is going to give you a chance – you do not have enough education to do what you envision – you cannot make it on your own." Doubt will talk you out of your great chances.

Doubt causes you to be overly skeptical of your future. When you are driven by doubt, instead of you looking at your future as being bright and rewarding, you begin to suspect that your future will be dark and nonproductive.

Face the fact, we all tend to encounter doubt from time to time, whether we are on the path of our compass or not. It is part of life. The question is when it comes to life compassing, will you allow your doubt to drive you, or will you be compass driven?

One of the interesting things about doubt is that it never goes away until you get rid of it. It never dies if you keep feeding it. If you never get rid of it, it can become a permanent fixture in your life. Not only does it stay. It will also rule your life. Even if you desire something better out of your life, you will never go for it because doubt convinces you that what you want is impossible to get, and instead of you leaping for what you want, you settle for just getting by and attempt to just make ends meet while hoping that things will change in your favor. As a result, you keep feeding your doubt. The more you feed it the larger and stronger it gets, and it demands more.

When you feed your doubt, it grows like the plant Audrey II in the 1986 movie and Broadway hit, "*The Little Shop of Horror*" that was fed raw meat and started desiring to eat humans. Throughout the movie and the play, the plant Audrey II would say to the owner of the shop, "Feed me, Seymour, feed me." Audrey II grows exceptionally large after being fed humans by Seymour. Audrey II ends up eating Seymour after destroying the shop. Doubt is like Audrey II, the more you feed it the more it wants, and over time it will end up eating you. It will eat up our dreams, ambitions, plans for success, gifts, and abilities. After these things are consumed by doubt, you will find yourself back into your nest and failing to soar the path of your compass and you end up never arriving at your True North.

When it comes to doubt, there are two types of people and we fit one of these types. There are those who allow their doubt to determine and dictate the path they take in life. Doubt becomes their compass regardless of them having the power and opportunity to choose what path they take. Doubt becomes the ruler of their destiny, and they never take the necessary leaps needed to progress into their future and to change things in their present. Those who doubt tend to give more attention to their weaknesses, limitations, flaws, and fears Then there are those who doubt their doubts. Those who doubt their doubts regardless of how strong the urge to doubt is, squash their doubts and they are determined to take the leap from their nest and follow their compass path that leads them to their destiny even though the risk may be involved. They tend to give more attention to their possibilities.

Even though we may be compass driven, knowing what our destiny is, and even filled with motivation, aspiration, and ambition to live the type of life we imagine and even have a plan to make it all happen, we are going to encounter doubt from time to time. So, do not let it surprise you or knock you off track. The question is, which type of person will you be during your bout with doubt? Will you squash your doubts, or will you let doubts squash you?

Here are some things you can do to help you squash your doubts:

+ *Admit when you are doubting. You cannot fight against what you do not acknowledge. Because you acknowledged something does not mean that it is permanent, and it cannot be changed.*
+ *Know the source of your doubt. Where is it coming from? Is it due to the way you have been taught? Is it due to the conversations you currently engage in? Is it due to you not having or taking the time to chill and you are tired and worn out? Whenever you are tired and worn out, you tend to doubt more than usual.*
+ *Make it a goal to develop your faith and practice it when you begin doubting. Remember that your faith can be greater than your doubt and can outdo your doubt.*
+ *When begin doubting, make the effort to fill your mind with positive thoughts no matter what situation you are in. Positive thoughts will help you maneuver through the maze of doubt.*
+ *Talk yourself out of doubting. It is a good thing for us to have people in our lives who encourages us to overcome our doubt, but we should never forget about the closest person to us who can talk us out of doubting, which is ourselves.*
+ *Pray about your doubt. Prayer can help you restore your hope and faith when you are dealing with situations that may cause you to doubt.*

AFFIRMATION #2

I am not ashamed of my past. I embrace it past with an open mind, an open heart, and with open arms. My past is what helps me appreciate my unique present. My past teaches me what I do not need for my future.

Part 2

Admitting Where You Have Been, and Accepting It

One of the hardest things to do is to admit where we have been because it resurfaces experiences in our lives that we prefer to keep buried, even though we know they exist. However, admitting where we have been, can be one of the most empowering things we can ever do if we let it. When we admit where we have been, we are empowered by knowing that our past is just that, the past, and we have no allegiance to it. One of the best gifts we can give ourselves, and that is to admit where we have been and saying goodbye to it, and step into our now as we embrace our great future.

Chapter 5

Facing Your Facts

*"The hardest part of living is making peace with your past.
Most of all, it's making peace with yourself."*

-Sherrilyn Kenyon

I used to hate facing the facts, particularly when it had something to do with my past failures, mistakes, and not so wise decisions. One of the common denominators that connects all people is that imperfection. The reality is that no one goes through life in perfect mode. No one is perfect in the affairs of life. This can be mind-blowing if one has set out to be a perfectionist.

I spent much of my life trying to be a perfectionist because I wanted to measure up to what others deem as "having it together." I realized that this was making me miserable because I knew deep down inside, I had flaws. As a result, when I made mistakes or failed at something, or made decisions, I covered it up and suffered alone, when I should have reached out for help. This made matters worse because I began finding ways to cope with my flaw, which caused me shame in my private world. I did not want to face the fact that I was not as perfect as I thought. I was way off my Life Compass and was taking paths that were never meant for me to take, and I was taking paths that were not leading me to my True North – my destiny for which I was created. Does this sound familiar?

My life changed when I grasped the reality that not facing the facts of my life journey was leading me to a dead end and keeping me off my truest path. As a result, I came into the light of reality. And that is the reality that everyone born into this world is prone to failures, mistakes, and not so wise decisions, and it is alright. It is part of the human equation.

<u>One of the most freeing things we can do is face the facts of our lives. When we make the decision and develop the courage to face the facts of our journey, we will discover that all the facts are not negative</u>. If we look hard enough at our journey, we will discover that some of our facts are positive. They just happen to be covered up by our negative facts. It is easier for us to give more attention and energy to the negative facts of life than the positive, and there are times we must dig ourselves out of the negative rubbish and discover the power of facing our facts regardless of how painful they may be.

If we never face the facts of our life, whether negative or positive, we never get to the next level of our better life. Facing the facts of our lives helps us to know where we have been as we attempt to live according to our Life Compass. As a matter of fact, our failures, mistakes, and not so wise decisions are part of Life Compassing. It is a matter of how we use them. I encourage you that as you develop a compass driven life that leads to your destiny to face the facts of your life. It is alright and you are alright because when you face the facts of your life, you discover what I term as "Divine Providence." <u>Divine Providence is the Creator taking the various events and experiences we have encountered in our lives, whether negative or positive, and weaving them into a beautiful tapestry for the world to see.</u> In other words, our facts of life are what the Creator uses to make us into the unique person we are. We just need to be willing to accept it. So, cry when you need to and laugh when you want to because it is all good. If we have breath, we have the chance to move life forward in a more rewarding way and direction. We come to the realization that we can rediscover who we are and begin to live according to our Life Compass as we aim towards our True North. As we follow our compass and go in the direction of our destiny we should do so while taking ownership of our story.

Owning Your Story

To go in the direction of our True North, which is our destiny, we must acknowledge that we can become a bestseller. We are living stories composed of experiences, encounters, circumstances, decisions, ideas, and aspirations. Our lives are stories in the process of being written, and we should make sure that we are the only ones holding the pen that writes our story. Be the author of your own story. **Do not allow anything or anybody to write your story for you. Be your own author. Regardless of what your story has been or is presently, own it and do not be ashamed of it, because your story is not all bad. It is your story, own it.** Each of our lives are stories in rough draft form. It is not complete. We are in the process of becoming a bestseller for the world to read. So, own your story out loud and in the light. By owning your story and with determination, positivity, and faith, your life can take the path that leads to your truest destiny.

When we approach owning our stories with determination, positivity, and faith and take the path that leads us to our truest destiny we discover that we step into the flow of divine providence. Divine Providence bespeaks of the Creator working all things together for our good. Even if we have experienced something negative, we will discover that these negative experiences have worked on our behalf and for our benefit, even though they were painful. Depending on our perspective, our painful experiences are what is needed for us to get back on our truest path and begin living according to our Life Compass. It is not always the good times that set us in the right direction, sometimes it is the hard strokes incurred in our life journey. Face the fact, each of our stories is composed of hard strokes that can bring out our truest portrait. Pablo Picasso once painted a portrait of Ambroise Vollard in the art style called "Cubism." When the portrait is viewed up close it is difficult to see the portrait because it is hidden by geometrical shapes and the hard strokes of the artist's brush along with many dark colors. However, when the viewer steps a distance away from the painting the portrait becomes clear to the eyes of the beholder. Our life story is composed of various strokes, colors, and shapes that tend to hide our truest portrait. If we would step a distance away from our circumstances, we will discover that our story has value and that it is our experiences that bring out the best in us if we will own our story. As we own our story, we will discover that it consists of failures. But our failures do not have to be the final chapter of our story.

Failures Are Not Final

As I faced the facts of my life and resolved to be intentional about identifying my Life Compass and my True North, I discovered an interesting temptation, and that is the temptation to believe that failures are final. This is due to the fact, that as seasons of success and accomplishments are etched into the walls of our memory, so are failures. Unfortunately, we have the tendency to remember our failures in more detail than our successes and accomplishments.

However, failures do not have to be final. We can bounce back from them. **To bounce back from failing is a matter of choice and will not happen automatically**.

We should remember a portion of a famous poetry quote by Alexander Pope, which says, "To err is human." This is to say that failure is a part of the human equation. Failure is a common denominator. It does not segregate or discriminate. Failure is part of human nature regardless of our position in life and what we have accomplished. We all fail at times, even at those things we are good at and have been doing well for years. We cannot always be on the top of our game. But because we are not always on top of our game does not mean our failures have to be final. Consider the basketball legend Michael Jordan. It has been said, "Michael Jordan missed a lot more than 9,000 shots in his career. According to Basketball Reference, he missed over 12,000 shots. But he also made more than 12,000 shots, scoring more than 32,000 points over the course of his career, putting him fifth on the all-time list. He ended his career with FG percentage of close to 500. And yes, Michael Jordan lost 366 regular games during the course of his career. But he won more than 700 regular season games, along with 119 playoff games." Failure does not have to be final. It depends on our determination to stay focused on winning and to keep playing the game as best we can and not get sidetracked because we lose some.

Failures do not necessarily suggest that we are not good at what we attempt to do, or not good enough, it simply implies that we are prone to momentary glitches in our humanity. Words of advice do not spend your time and day trying to prove to people that you are alright. The truth is, we will never satisfy everybody, and some people will never know or accept our worth and value no matter how hard we try to impress them. Whether we fail at something or not, we will never be accepted and valued by everyone we encounter in life. So, do not allow anyone to press you to the point where you do not have room to err. This makes for a very frustrating life. When we live in frustration, we tend to get off our Life Compass and risk missing arriving at our True North.

Many people live in frustration and get sidetracked off their Life Compass and risk missing arriving at their True North while blowing fuses and blowing circuits because they have not accepted the fact that they are not perfect. The best that they can do is to shoot for excellence and leave some room for error. In this way, they will not be so uptight when they fail at something.

Along with me, many people attempt to live according to our Life Compass and aim to arrive at our True North, the best we can do is to shoot for excellence versus perfection. Let me explain, excellence refers to something a person excels in. Excel means to rise above something or surpass something or to be better or greater than something. On the other hand, perfect or perfection indicates that something or someone is faultless, flawless, or complete in all aspects without defect. The fact is we can be excellent in excelling above and beyond something without being perfect. But to advance towards excellence, we must not allow our failures to be greater than our confidence and faith. If our confidence and faith are not greater than our failures, we will not rebound from our failures. **Many people live in the shadows of their failures and not in the light of their possibilities.** If we do not rebound from our failures and learn from them, we run the risk of becoming what we did in our past or staying in what we did not do. This is to say that we will end up becoming a failure because we failed. This does not have to be the case. Failure is not the worst thing in life. It only becomes one of the worst things when we allow it to determine the remainder of our lives and dictate whether, or not we reach our God given destiny. We should be determined never to let our failures be our destination.

From a positive perspective, failure can sometimes be exactly what we need, because when we experience failure and learn from it, it causes us to re-evaluate ourselves, and how we do things, as well as how we respond to the various events and circumstances of life. It also gives us a chance to reinvent ourselves. It can be a good thing depending on how we use it versus it using us. It helps us to know what not to spend our time doing, as well as what we are weak and strong in. In a nutshell, our failure does not have to be final. It can be used to get us on the path of our Life Compass and press us closer to our True North. Our failures do not have to be wasted.

Don't Waste Your Failures

Failures are not final, and they do not have to be the end of it all. Failures are only final when we allow them to be.

Unfortunately, many people allow their failures to dictate and determine how they live their lives after they have failed. I know this firsthand and not by theory or by other people's experiences.

There have been times in my life when I believed that because I had failed at something, whether it was something that I had the potential to do well, or something that I should have restrained myself from doing, but did it anyway, I was a failure. I often held to this belief because of how others treated me when I failed. We have all had such experiences. The truth of the matter is that when it comes to us failing, not all people will look beyond our failures and see our potential, even though they are as human as we are and capable of failing. This had a negative effect on my psychological world as it concerned how I viewed myself, as well as my emotional and spiritual world after having failed at something.

Psychologically, when I failed, I thought of myself as not being worthy of anything better than what I was receiving. As a result, I began to think that when something happened negatively, I was being punished because of my failures.

Emotionally, When I failed, I found myself trying to correct the things I failed at for the acceptance and pleasing of others, to prove to them that I was not a bad person. This became very emotionally draining.

Spiritually, I found myself distancing myself from God who I know is my source of power, who empowers me to live my life at its best. This was due to how people who said that they were close to God treated people including myself who failed. Therefore, I began to feel that maybe God felt the same way about me as well as other people who failed.

As a result of these experiences, each day when I woke up, I aimed not to fail versus aiming at living the life I was given and aim at living it well. Sometimes we can be so busy trying not to fail, that we end up never winning. I came to realize that no matter how hard we try not to fail at something, failure is inevitable at times. It is part of the human equation, and it is alright.

One day I woke up and realized that I could accept my failures and that I did not have to waste them and that they could help me begin living the life I can live well. We can use our failures as allies versus enemies, and they can help us get on our compass path, maintain it, as well as help us arrive at our destiny.

This is not to say that we should settle for failing. We should never accept failure as a permanent fixture in our lives. However, when we fail, we must not allow ourselves to be beaten so far down that we begin to live like failures. We can embrace our failures and learn from them and use them for our benefit. Our failures do not have to be wasted. They can work for us if we work them in a positive manner. Since we are going to fail at times, we might as well use them for our benefit.

Here are some positive benefits that come from your failures when you use them instead of wasting them.

Your failures can help you come to grips with your areas of weakness and vulnerability.

Your failures can help you become more focused on your strengths.

Your failures can help you identify what works and what does not work for you.

Your failures can help you identify who truly value you regardless of how well you perform in life.

Your failures help you recognize those who do not truly values you unless you perform well according to their standards and beliefs.

Your failures help you draw closer to your source of power that empowers you to live your best life.

Chapter 6
Stop Punishing Yourself

"Be willing to stop punishing yourself for your mistakes. Love yourself for your willingness to learn and grow."

-Louise Hay

Parker Palmer states in his book entitled, *The Courage to Teach*, that "No punishment anyone lays on you could possibly be worse than the punishment you lay on yourself by conspiring in your own diminishment." If we are honest with ourselves, we can admit that we all have self-inflicted experiences that tend to keep us nailed to our past failures, mistakes, and not so wise decisions. These self-inflicted experiences can sometimes cause us to punish ourselves in some way or another, which causes us to sometimes get off our Life Compass. Such punishment can be draining. It drains us emotionally while casting shadows that prevent us from living in the light of our present existence.

When you are busy punishing yourself, you tend to linger in your negative past and forget that your past has not been all negative. When you overlook the fact that all your past has not been totally negative, you fail to celebrate your accomplishments by which you remain under some dark cloud of your past that can cause you to take paths that do not coincide with your compass, hoping to escape your reality. When you are busy punishing yourself, you can feel unworthy of greater things and a greater life. When this occurs, you can develop unhealthy habits that can delay your arrival at your True North – your destiny. In addition, when you are busy punishing yourself, you tend to diminish your value and worth. **<u>You can never reach for the stars in your life while feeling unworthy of the stars</u>**. As a result, instead of following your compass that leads to your destiny, you can find yourself sitting on some curb in your journey with unused potential. I contend that one of the ways to break the cycle of self-punishment is through self-forgiveness.

The Power of Self-Forgiveness

I grew up in church and was taught the importance of forgiving others. But I do not remember ever being taught how to forgive myself for my own failures, mistakes, or bad decisions. Even though I prayed and asked God for forgiveness and believed that He did, something was still missing. I was still carrying guilt and shame. As a result, instead of me being busy following my compass and going for my destiny, I was busy trying to correct history. As you very well know that we can never correct history or relive it because history is history whether it is negative or positive. Whenever we are busy trying to correct history, we become stuck in our past and stagnant in our present which delays our arriving at the destiny for which we are designed and equipped. Unforgiveness has a power over us that keeps us from using our fullest potential. We cannot follow our compass and arrive at our destiny without using our potential.

I finally decided to take the time and go back to the basic meaning of forgiveness. Which is to develop a disposition or willingness to forgive someone by which they are set free and pardoned. I concluded that if forgiving others can work for them in a positive matter, then forgiving myself can work for me as well. Once I started making a journey towards self-forgiveness, I discovered how powerful it is and how it helps us to regain our balance and get back on the path of our Life Compass. I contend that it is almost impossible to keep balance while following the path of our life compass because the load of unforgiveness throws us off balance and drains our energy, as well as draws attention back to the past and we fail to focus our attention on our positive present and the awesome possibilities of our future.

Once we engage in forgiving ourselves, we discover that we are no longer obligated to yesterday, but become obligated to the present. When we forgive ourselves, we let go of unneeded and unnecessary baggage that has kept us from going for our destiny as we follow the path of our Life Compass. Self-forgiveness has the power to set us free to use our potential, abilities, and giftedness. These are important to maintain our balance and focus as we live compass driven. Self-forgiveness also empowers us to get a fresh perspective of ourselves that has been hidden in the shadows of unforgiveness. It also helps us to realize that even though we have flaws we are not as bad as we think. Once these things are discovered, we can become excited again about living our best life possible.

I suggest the following regarding embracing the power of Self-forgiveness as you live compass driven:

+ *Grasp the realization that no one is perfect, and that we all have flaws and are subject to mistakes, failures, and making no so wise decisions. It is part of our humanity.*

+ *Do not spend your energy trying to correct the past, because it is impossible to correct the past. The events of our past are etched in history and cannot be changed.*

+ *Stop reliving your negative past. When you relive your negative past, it delays your arrival at your destiny.*
+ *Take the time to take inventory of your best qualities. Regardless of what your past may be, you are not all bad. There is some awesome goodness in you.*
+ *Give yourself permission to let go of your negative past. There are times when we hold on to our negative past until we give ourselves permission to let it go.*

Drop the Buckets!

After discovering the power of self-forgiveness and making an honest attempt to get back on the path of my Life Compass, I discovered another fact, perhaps you can relate. And that is the tendency to carry what I call "Buckets" even though we have been forgiven and have forgiven ourselves. I define "Buckets" as those negative weighty experiences that pop up in our mind and emotions from time to time that can become a driving force as to how we view life and how we attempt to live our lives. **"Buckets" can become the determining factor as to how we view our future. They can determine how we view our present, as well as whether we see our future as positive or negative.**

I discovered that some of the buckets we tend to carry and hold on to have been handed down to us from generations, perhaps by the way we were taught as kids, the community we grew up in, the household we grew up in, certain mindsets and belief systems that we have accepted as being the norm.

There are times when the buckets we carry, whether mentally or emotionally, dictate how we maneuver on the path of our Life Compass. Even though we do not like carrying them we tend to pick them up day after day. If we would do an analysis of ourselves, we will discover that we all carry unnecessary buckets at some point. We just call them baggage. As we live compass driven, one of the awesome tasks and challenges we all face is, whether we release the buckets we are carrying or continue to carry them. This is a matter of choice. We may not have control over the buckets that life tends to throw our way or hang on us, but we do have the power to choose whether we carry them or not. We can choose to put them down and not allow them to dictate how we maneuver as we are being compass driven. It is not always easy to put buckets down and let them go because the truth of the matter is, that buckets can become addictive, particularly if we do not have anything positive to replace them with. Even though it is sometimes difficult to release buckets and let them go, it can be accomplished with a bit of hard work.

When you resolve to live according to your Life Compass and aim towards your True North, I offer the following suggestions that can help you release your buckets:

Acknowledge that you are carrying buckets. Buckets do not go away because you do not acknowledge them. The best way to get over something is to first admit that it exists.

If possible, try to identify where they came from. Buckets come from somewhere. They just do not appear. Name them. Every bucket has a name and a description. To release them you must know what you call them.

Resolve that you do not desire to carry them any longer. We will never let go of our buckets until we make up our minds that we no longer want them.

Come up with a workable plan that will help you release them. Releasing anything that is not good for you takes planning, particularly if it has been a part of your life for a long period of time.

Be intentional about releasing them. Releasing buckets does not happen automatically. Depending on the size of the bucket and how long we have been carrying them, it will take some hard work, determination, and intentionality.

Accepting Yourself

One of the things that can help you drop the buckets you tend to carry is getting to a point during your compass journey where you accept yourself. If we are honest, we all can admit that there are times when accepting who we are and where we have been in our journey is one of the hardest things to do. This is due to the fact, that there are some things in our past that we rather forget and sweep under the carpet out of our sight, as well as out of the sight of others. Accepting who we are and who we are created to be is a hard task at times because we realize that we are flawed, and we tend to measure our quality or how good we are doing by others' perceptions. We live in an impressive society. We have an inner longing to impress others. I contend that this is largely due to the fact that we fail to accept who we are and where we have been. I am always amazed at how we can identify with the uniqueness of others and celebrate them with their flaws while bypassing and rejecting our uniqueness, because of our flaws. I have discovered in my own journey that it is easier to love and celebrate others for who they are regardless of their past than it is for us to love and celebrate ourselves with our past. We often cheer others on and forget to cheer ourselves on. This is because we have trouble accepting who we are. As the old saying goes, "We think that other folk's grass is greener."

Living a compass driven life and going for our True North – our destiny is about accepting who we are, flaws and all that comes with it. Living according to our compass is not about perfectivity, versus it being about being persistent in our journey towards our True North. Life compassing demands that we accept who we are. Our compass is tailored to who we are authentically. Life will never be all it is intended to be until we arrive at the point of accepting ourselves without condemnation. When we condemn ourselves, we tend to despise our path, because we believe that those who are on a good path are flawless, which is far from the truth. **Be encouraged to follow your Life Compass and accept who you are and where you have been because this is a part of your awesome uniqueness**.

Here are several things you can do as it pertains to accepting yourself:

+ *Learn to love yourself for who you are, regardless of your past and flaws. Remember that no one is perfect.*
+ *Imagine who you can become and what you can accomplish if you accept who you are. Remember that no one is totally bad.*
+ *Imagine what you and the world will miss in the future if you do not accept yourself. There is something that only you can do in the world. No one else can do it.*
+ *Practice encouraging yourself with positive powerful affirmations concerning you. Our best encourager is ourselves.*
+ *If you do not like something about yourself, change it. Most of the things about us are changeable if we have the discipline and courage to change them.*

Chapter 7

Bouncing Back from Disappointments

"One's best success comes after their greatest disappointments."
-Henry Ward Beecher

"Success is how high you bounce after you hit bottom."
-General George Patton

L ife is sometimes painted with disappointments. Experiencing disappointments in life is one of the common denominators in life that is inescapable. If we are not careful to bounce back from them, they can knock us off our Life Compass and we risk missing arriving at our appointed destiny. I have discovered and learned during my own journey that I cannot go through life without experiencing disappointments. To this day, for me, and maybe you can relate, and that is experiencing disappointments in any form and from any source is a hard pill to swallow at times. Even though it is a hard pill to swallow, it is imperative that we bounce back from them to start living a compass driven life or remain compass driven by which we arrive at our True North.

Bouncing back from our disappointments to the degree that they have no power over us, we must be intentional. Bouncing back from disappointments does not happen automatically. We must bounce back from our disappointments no matter how far back or how recent they occurred, or it becomes impossible to take hold holistically of the great possibilities that are present in our lives and lay ready to be taken hold of in our future. **One of the hardest arts to learn is bouncing back from disappointments and overcoming them.** Life is composed of disappointments in some form or another. Disappointments are universal. It does not discriminate or segregate. It is unpredictable, for if we could detect disappointments coming, we would guard ourselves against them. But this is not the case. Because disappointments are undetectable ahead of time, it is easy for us to be thrown off our Life Compass, and it can shock us to the point that we forget about our True North. This is one of the reasons that when it occurs, we must be intentional about making an honest effort to bounce back from them as soon as possible. One of the worse things we can do after being disappointed, and is to waddle in the experience. Now, do not get me wrong, I am not a master of not waddling in my disappointments. However, I have arrived at the conclusion, that to waddle in our disappointments can have a negative effect on us in several ways. All of which can determine how we live compass driven and get to our True North.

Not having the coping skills or strategies to bounce back from disappointments effectively can threaten your emotional health, physical wellbeing, and your psychological wellness, resulting in symptoms such as depression, anger, apathy, denial, and fear. I know firsthand that when these symptoms take root in our lives it becomes almost impossible if not completely impossible to live compass driven and stay pointed and moving in the direction of our True North. I offer you the following strategies that may help us bounce back from our disappointing experiences as we make an honest attempt to live according to our Life Compass and stay focused in the direction of our True North. Consider the following:

Face the truth of the situation. Denying the reality of a disappointing experience does not help the situation. As the saying goes, "the truth will set you free." Even if it hurts.

Give yourself permission to mourn the disappointing experience. Depending on our perspective of mourning, it can be a cleansing and healthy approach to getting past disappointments.

Do not get stuck feeling and treating yourself like a victim. We will never get beyond disappointments and take a victor's stance while being stuck with having a victim mentality, even if we have been victimized.

Check to see if your expectation of the situation or the person who disappointed you is realistic. Even if your expectation was realistic, we must keep in mind that situations or persons are not flawless.

Be kind to yourself. Being down on yourself will not help you rise to the place you are supposed to be or are capable of being.

Look for the lesson in the situation. Every disappointing experience has a lesson in it. We can use these lessons to help us move forward beyond disappointment.

Get back in your game. Sitting on the sidelines and waddling in the mud of your disappointments will not help you feel better. As a matter of fact, it makes us feel worse because we continue to relive the situation that caused us disappointment.

Resilience

One of the things that help us bounce back from disappointments is resilience. Staying the path of our Life Compass and finding our True North takes resilience. No one can stay the path of their compass and remain focused on their destiny without being resilient. A common definition of resilience is having the ability to bounce back or to spring back into original the shape or appointed position. It is the ability to recover strength, spirit, and to become buoyant. **My personal definition of resilience is someone having the ability, tenacity, faith, and courage to bounce back into their original and designed shape, as well as get back on the path that leads to their destiny, after being twisted or bent out of shape by their situation, circumstances, and misfortunes, whether they were caused simply by life events, by others or self-inflicted.** Resilience is one's refusal to stay on the bottom when the pressures of life press us down. It is having the faith and boldness in the strength of the Creator to keep springing back into shape when we have been bent out of shape and torn by the events of life.

I have discovered in my own life journey, that has been sometimes painted with disappointments, setbacks, and not so favorable events, whether by way of the natural flow of life, or by those who I thought had my best interest but did not, or by my own unwise decisions and flaws, that resilience gives us the power to bounce back into position despite what we have experienced, and gives us the strength we need to laugh about it, as well as use them as learning moments.

Resiliency is to be buoyant. It is having the determination to float back to the surface when we have been weighed down by some unfortunate encounter. It is our ability to ride and float on the ripples of life.

Resilience is having the faith and the ability to take the chance to try something again that we failed at or to attempt something different, even if it bends us out of shape or out of our comfort zone while knowing that the Creator is in total control of our destiny and will not allow us to be bent beyond our ability to bounce back into shape.

Resilience is imperative as it pertains to living compass driven and maintaining our path that leads to our True North. Without being resilient, it becomes easy for us to be knocked off the path of our compass.

Regardless of how intentional and determined we are to follow the path of our Life Compass, as well as being focused on our True North, there will be times when things occur, that will draw our attention, focus, and energy. As it relates to being compass driven and focused on our destiny, when our attention, focus, and energy are drawn in another direction, we can become easily bent out of shape and thrown off our true path. Therefore, it is imperative that we practice resilience that enables us to bounce back and continue our true path. I contend that without resilience being one of our characteristics it becomes almost impossible, if not totally impossible to stay the path of our Life Compass and continue to move towards our True North.

There are several things we can do to build a resilient character that will help us remain on the path of our compass and help us stay focused on our destiny.

Strengthen Your Resilience Muscle: Developing a resilient character is not easy. But it can be accomplished with intention, determination, and some hard work. There is no perfect formula for developing our resilience muscle. Strengthening our resilience muscle is not about avoiding the stress that we sometimes experience as we follow our compass but learning how to manage it. We can strengthen our resilience muscle by practicing the art of mindfulness. Mindfulness is a state or quality of being mindful or aware of the present moment. Psychologically speaking, mindfulness is a technique in which one focuses their full attention only on the present while experiencing thoughts, feelings, and sensations without judging them. Regarding living compass driven, our resilience muscle is strengthened when we take the time to focus our attention on the positive aspects of the challenges we are faced with through meditation.

Master an Optimistic Outlook: We all face challenges from time to time that can throw us off our path if we allow them to define us and dictate our response. We must keep in mind that our challenges do not define us no matter how challenging they are. What defines us is how we respond to our challenges. Being optimistic is not about falsifying our challenges, but realizing that they are real, but not allowing them to throw us off balance. When we maintain an optimistic outlook that is realistic, yet positive, we can maneuver positively during our challenges by which we stay the path of our compass and stay focused on our destiny. One of the best things we can do as we face various challenges while following the path of our compass is not to deny the negatives of the challenge but maintain a positive focus on what is in our control.

Overcome Your Doubt: Disappointments can cause us to doubt whether the path of our compass and our destiny is really for us. When we are in doubt mode, we tend not to be resilient, and we stay in the shape our negative experience has put us. To become resilient, we must be intentional and deliberate about practicing positive self-Affirmations.

Practice Forgiving Others: When it comes to being resilient and living compass driven and staying focused in the direction of our destiny, forgiveness plays a major role. Often, we can get stuck in resentment that tends to keep us shackled to our past negative experiences. Living with unforgiveness tends to draw our focus off what is most imperative for us to move forward. It is not always the negative experiences, pain, and hurt that we have encountered that keep us from living according to our compass or knock us off the course of our compass, sometimes it's our inability or our reluctance to forgive. We must keep in mind that when we do not forgive, we give those who have caused us pain, and the events that have caused us pain to have control over us, which can dictate how I move according to our Life Compass and how we remain focused on our True North.

Finding Your Way Back to You

With all the challenges and disappointments, we face, life can become an interesting journey that causes us to lose ourselves and be thrown off our compass, and begin focusing on things other than what we are created for. We sometimes lose and misplace things that we deem important to us. The most important thing we can lose, is ourselves. Have you ever lost yourself? How long has it been since you have seen the real you? **If you tapped yourself on**

<u>the shoulder, would you recognize yourself?</u> It could be "Yes," or it could be "No." We lose ourselves at times when we allow ourselves to be thrown off our compass by our challenges and disappointments. When we lose ourselves, we lose our authenticity, self-esteem, self-perception, and our style. When these are misplaced, our lives become more hectic, and we take paths that are not meant for us because we have no self-connection. There is a path that only we can take and a place that only we can arrive at. But we can never take that path and maintain it or arrive at our appointed destiny until we connect to ourselves. There are steps that can lead us back to ourselves, but it takes tenacity.

Acknowledge: Face the fact when you have lost yourself. The only way we can find something is by first acknowledging that it is no longer in our possession. Being compass driven and knowing what you want in life is not about never losing ourselves. But when we lose ourselves and acknowledge it, we are then able to get back on our path.

Acceptance: Receive the real you back to you, even if others do not. Do not mask yourself from you. We can never be resilient when we do not accept ourselves, flaws, and all.

Permission: Give yourself permission to come back to you and be all that you are to yourself. There are times when it is imperative that we give ourselves permission to return to ourselves.

Thankfulness: Always be thankful for who you are despite your flaws. When we are thankful for who we are, we are careful not to let ourselves go so quickly and easily.

Responsibility: Take one hundred percent responsibility for getting yourself back. Don't wait for others to find you. Go after yourself and bring yourself back to where you belong and are created to be.

Getting Past What You Can't Get Over

There's good news, and the good news is, we can live an enjoyable and empowered life beyond our negative past, regardless of how long ago or how recent the occurrence, even if we are not over them. We can live past the things we cannot get over.

I have heard and have even said, and perhaps you have as well, to people as it pertains to something or someone that they were having an issue with and that is to "Get over it." But the fact is, that there are some experiences and episodes that occur in life that we cannot simply get over, depending on the experience and how it was experienced.

There are some experiences that occur in life that are not just projected on the screens of our minds, but they are chiseled in the walls of our memory and are permanent and cannot be deleted.

Each of us has painful and disappointing experiences whether they are self-inflicted, caused by others, or by natural circumstances, that we are not able to get over.

I used to believe that to live the life I am created to live successfully, I had to get over every negative experience that has happened or currently happening in my life. But I came to the realization that I do not necessarily have to get over every negative event that has occurred or is occurring, versus me getting past them and begin living my life according to my Life Compass, as well as remaining focused on what I believe is my True North, regardless of them.

Beyond religious beliefs and how we were taught, if we are honest, we will admit that there are some things in our lives that we have the tendency not to get over, regardless if we desire to or not. They can become like can be like permanent fixtures in a house. They come with the structure, whether we like it or not. Not getting over something is not necessarily a sign of a lack of faith or power over a situation. It simply means that we are human and that we cannot remove the history that have been etched in our minds. As a matter of fact, I personally care not to forget every painful and disappointing experience I have encountered because when I remember them, I also remember how I was blessed to get through them and the victory over them, by which I am built, empowered and made stronger to conquer more as I live compass driven. Not getting over something simply denotes the fact that we are merely human and not super-human even though we have faith.

As you live compass driven, you will discover that even though there are some things that you cannot get over, you can get past them to the point that they have no power over your present or your future.

We may not be able to remove experiences from our minds, we can remove ourselves out of the experience and move on and begin living according to our compass and live successfully. To remove ourselves out of those experiences that has caused us pain and disappointment is to not allow those experiences, pains, and disappointments to have power over us and to dictate our disposition and how we take the path of our compass.

Removing ourselves from a painful and disappointing experience does not happen automatically. It takes intention to move past them. We must be intentional about walking out of it and waving goodbye to it, which says to it, "You are no-longer a part of my life to the point that you affect me."

The question is, what are you saying good morning to as you start your day? Our days can be ruled by that which we welcome to be a part of our day. If we welcome our past pains and disappointments in our daily lives, they will go with us throughout the day and have power over us. Even though we cannot help but remember painful and disappointing experiences we do not have to lay a welcome mat out for them to come in and out of our lives and rule how we live. We can remember something or somebody, but we do not have to have breakfast, lunch, and dinner with it or them. We can move past them even if we are not over them.

To get past something is about admitting that it exists, but not allowing it to affect your present condition of existence, nor how you perform in life. Admitting that something exists is a first step towards getting past it. We can never get past something until we acknowledge that something is present, and it prevents us from moving forward. One of the ways to move on from something is by looking it square in the face and letting it know that we see it, but not afraid of it.

To get past something is having the scars and proof of our painful and disappointing experiences without letting it affect the type of life we live. I have scars on my left ankle caused by an accident back in the eighties. I see these scars every day, and they remind me of the accident. However, I do not relive the accident. To get past something is remembering an experience, but not reliving it.

To get past what we cannot get over as we live compass driven while aiming at our True North, it is imperative that we recognize the signs of not getting past what we cannot get over.

Signs of not getting past what we cannot get over:

+ **Our disposition—mentally, emotionally, physically, and spiritually is altered when we think about certain negative experiences.** There were times when I would think about some of my past experiences, and my whole disposition would change almost instantly. My mind would be filled with negative and defeating thoughts – I would become sad – my whole demeaner would change and was noticeable by others and my faith would drop low.

+ **We all have the tendency to fall into some form of depression when we think about negative experiences.** All depression is not major. But depression is depression whether minor or major. There was a time when I was on a journey of depression. I discovered that my depression was not due to something I was experiencing currently, but it was because I was still holding on to my negative past or it was holding on to me, because I had not discovered that I did not have to get over my past, versus me getting past it.

+ **We continue to live as if we are still in the negative experience.** I was always fascinated with elephants – their size and awesome strength. But what fascinated me the most was how they would swing one leg back and forth, particularly if they were in a zoo or a circus. I came to realize that one of the reasons the elephant constantly swings their leg is because when they were young and had no idea of their awesome strength they were trained while being chained to a peg in the ground. As a result, even though the young elephant has grown to massive size and strength, and is capable of escaping its domain, it continues to relive how it was trained which caused them to spend time swinging their leg versus using its size and strength to get free. When we fail to understand that we do not have to get over our negative experiences but just get past them, we live tied to our negative past, and we never use our abilities, power, and mental capacities to escape our captive domains.

I love the Scripture, Philippians 3:13b (NIV), which says, *"But one thing I do: Forgetting what is behind and straining toward what is ahead."* Even though we may not be able to get over some of the negative experiences we have encountered, even those that currently exist, we can get past them, and here is how.

+ **Forget those negative things that are behind you.** This is not suggesting that we do not remember what we have gone through. It does suggest that we cut the umbilical cord that is connected to our negative past that prevents us from living our best present and from embracing our awesome future. One of the purposes of the umbilical cord that is connected to the mother and the fetus is for the fetus to receive nourishment from the mother. If we are strongly connected to what we cannot get over, versus getting past it we are constantly fed by them which can prevent us from living compass driven and we risk not arriving at our destiny at least in a timely manner.

+ **Put forth an honest effort with laser focus toward what is in front of you.** We can never get a clear perspective of our future and our present possibilities without focusing on what is in front of us. Do not drive through the rest of your life using your rearview mirror, you will run into something and miss what is in front of you.

+ **Recognize your source of strength that empowers you to get past what you cannot get over.** There is a source of power that is available to each of us if we are willing to tap into it. In my own journey I came to realize that because I am not always humanly capable of getting past some events that have occurred in my life, I needed to tap into a higher source. For me, it is God the Creator of the universe. For you, your source of strength may be something or someone else. But whatever and whoever your source of strength may be, tap into it and receive what you need to get past what you cannot get over.

+   **Resolve that you want to be strong enough to get past what you cannot get over.** Being and acting weak can be addictive because it keeps us from taking the responsibility of letting go of some painful and disappointing experience that we have become accustomed to, and comfortable with even though we do not like how it feels. It is psychological. Therefore, we must make the decision that we will muster up the strength we need to move forward on the path of our compass.

+   **Recognize that you have been equipped with what you need to get past what you cannot get over.** Have confidence in your abilities to get past something in your life. If no one else believes in you, believe in yourself. Others believing in us is not what really matters, believing in ourselves and our abilities is what really counts.

Chapter 8
Measuring Yourself

"The real contest is always between what you've done and what you're capable of doing. You measure yourself against yourself and nobody else."

-Geoff Gaberino

One of the greatest temptations we face is to measure ourselves according to who others are and what they have accomplished. As I looked back over my life and take an honest and serious inventory of my journey, I discovered that I spent much time and energy measuring my successes and accomplishments by the successes and accomplishments of others. This was not intentional versus me allowing myself to be shaped by the urge to compare myself to others. Possibly you can relate. I contend that due to social media and commercialism we are easily drawn to compare ourselves with others and their successes and what they have accomplished. In my opinion, comparing ourselves to others is a form of measurement. Please do not get me wrong, we can learn from the successes and accomplishments of others, and it can have a positive effect if we do not allow ourselves to be drawn into comparing ourselves with them. Learning from others' successes and accomplishments is different from comparing ourselves with them.

Learning from others' successes and accomplishments can teach us various ways and techniques as to how to accomplish our own dreams. However, when we begin to compare ourselves with others, we begin to acquiesce to who they are, what they are doing, and how they are living their lives which causes us to begin to measure ourselves with them.

If one is not careful, time and energy can be spent attempting to do what others have done and missing what we should be doing. It is good to have role models or people we admire and learn from, but not to the extent that we spend our time and energy trying to be them. This causes us to not live in our own authenticity and creativity.

No human is created the same, even though we have some similarities. The Creator has created us differently and for a particular purpose, that only we can perform, even if it resembles something that someone else is doing or has accomplished. After all, there is nothing new under the sun. **One of our tasks in life is to discover what we have to offer to the world.** The best we can do is to learn from others as it pertains to learning new methods on how to get something accomplished but mastering something depends on our own authenticity. Romans 12:3 (NIV), says, *"Do not think of yourself more highly than you ought, but rather think of yourself with sober judgement."* I agree that we should not think of ourselves more highly than we ought. But, on the other hand, we should not think too low of ourselves that we begin measuring ourselves by others and to other people's lives. Marianne Williamson in her book entitled, *A Return to Love,* says the following, "Our deepest fear is not that we are inadequate. Our deepest fear is that we are powerful beyond measure. It is our light, not our darkness that most frighten us. We ask ourselves, "Who am I to be brilliant, gorgeous, talented, fabulous?" Actually, who are you not to be? You are a child of God.

You're playing small does not serve the world. There is nothing enlightening about shrinking..." **Measuring ourselves to others is a way of playing small and shrinking**. We can never stay the path of our Life Compass and go for our True North while playing small and shrinking.

To follow our Life Compass and to stay in the direction of our True North, it is imperative that we practice measuring ourselves. Self-Measuring is about getting a clear view of who we are and created to be while taking into consideration our abilities, potential, purpose, and giftedness, and using them to help us stay on our course of life, without comparing or measuring ourselves to others. To accomplish this, we must know our worth and value, as well as know what does not fit us.

Knowing Your Worth

When we practice measuring ourselves the chances are we will come to know our worth. There are lots of "Self" words, phrases, and topics that have unique qualities that assist us in how to live our best life. One of the most powerful "Self" words, phrases, and topics in my opinion is "Self-Worth." Self-Worth is defined as being aware and clear about the level of importance we place on ourselves. It can be considered as an emotional outlook concerning how we feel about ourselves that determines how and what we feel about ourselves in comparison to others.

Self-Worth is an imperative fundamental part of our condition of existence that determines our perspective of us that is detached from the perspective of others about us. Self-Worth is having a healthy picture of ourselves despite our immediate circumstances, and how others may perceive us. Self-Worth is not about us seeing ourselves as better than others, versus it simply being about us embracing our uniqueness while knowing that others are unique as well.

Unfortunately, many people view their Self-Worth based upon their accumulation of material things. Even though the accumulation of things may play a vital role in our lives, they do not define who we are or our truest worth. Our truest worth is not about how much we have as it pertains to material things, versus it being about who we are created to be and how we view ourselves. When our perspective of ourselves is based upon materialism, when we lose these things, it can have a major negative effect on us that can sometimes determine how we live our lives and what we expect from life, as well as from ourselves. I know this all too well.

After having experienced material setbacks during my journey, I started feeling worthless and that caused me to go into depression. It also caused me to abandon the goals I had set for myself, as well as attempt to take paths that were not intended for me. This caused me to take the road of least resistance and simply settle for whatever life threw me. However, I came to the reality that material things did not make me and that my worth was not based upon how much I had, versus it being based upon who God had made me be, and God does not make messes. He makes masterpieces. After coming to grips with this reality, I set out to rebuild my life and get back to evaluating myself from a healthy perspective. As a result, I'm happy to say that I live more compass driven and intentional about staying focused on the destiny for which I am created. My friends, you can do the same. You can recover a healthy perspective of yourself no matter what your condition of existence may be, with some hard work and intentional focusing.

When it comes to our Life Compass and being focused on our True North, it is important that we have a healthy perspective and picture of ourselves. When we have a healthy perspective and picture of ourselves, we are encouraged to follow our best path that leads to our destiny. When we understand and embrace our uniqueness, we discover that we are built for more and that we deserve to live the type of life we are created to live. When we arrive at this point in our journey, we are encouraged to set out on our truest path according to our life Compass and get to our True North. As we set our lives according to our Life Compass, there are several things we can do to embrace and develop our Self-Worth.

Get a clear understanding of your attitude about yourself. How we perceive ourselves and how we present ourselves, becomes reality. Our thoughts and attitudes are like magnets, they draw to us what we think about the most and what we give our emotions to most. Attitude is not just emotions that are also thoughts. As a man thinks, so he becomes over time. Sometimes this happens without him knowing it is occurring. It is not about the attitude others have towards us that really counts and determines the type of life we live. It is our attitude towards ourselves that really matters in the whole scheme of things.

Develop a healthy perspective of Self-Love. We really cannot love others until we first love ourselves. Unfortunately, people who display Self-Love are often considered narcissistic or egotistical. This is not always the case. We can have Self-Love without being narcissistic or egotistical when it is handled properly. We can have a healthy perspective of Self-Love and be humble while embracing the awesome uniqueness of others. When we develop and embrace a healthy perspective of Self-Love, we see ourselves as the person we have been created to be and not cheat ourselves out of the best of life. When we love ourselves, we will attempt to give ourselves the best that life offers.

Honestly Analyze Yourself. It is important to practice analyzing ourselves and be honest about what we find. When we honestly analyze ourselves, we do not just discover what is wrong with us. We also discover what is good and right about us. When we are honest with ourselves, we identify those things that need improving or let go of. We also identify those wonderful things about us that we can cultivate for a better life. If we cannot be honest first with ourselves, it becomes almost impossible to really be honest with others. If you are going to be honest with someone, let you be the first person you are honest with. When we are honest with ourselves, we discover our real worth.

Don't let your Self-Worth be Contingent on other People. When we attempt to live according to other people's expectations of us, versus living according to our own expectations, we find it a struggle to meet their standards which can sometimes be unrealistic. Some people mean us well, but our Self-Worth is really based upon our own expectations of us, which is our foundation.

Matter to yourself. We must remember that we should matter to ourselves, even if we do not matter to others. We should matter to ourselves more than we matter to others. We should practice on a regular basis affirming to ourselves as to how much we matter, as well remember that we are important to the world. Every life matters.

Practice building your Self-Confidence. Even though it is rewarding when others believe in us, it is more important that we believe in ourselves. To build consciousness of our Self-Worth, we must build our confidence. We can do this by reminding ourselves of our abilities, potential, and giftedness and not comparing them

101

to others, and by emptying our minds of negative thoughts concerning us.

Break the habit of being a people pleaser. We all like impressing others and having them feel good about us because we are social creatures. We are made to feel secure when others are pleased with us. We can desire for others to like or even love us so badly, that we waste time and energy trying to please them more than being satisfied with our lives. Sometimes this is done at our expense with no reward, and we dim our light for their satisfaction. When we stop trying to please others at the expense of our and becoming a zero, we will begin to rise to the surface and can start working towards building the consciousness of our worth and happiness.

Knowing Your Cadence

We are all born with a cadence, whether we know it or not. You will find it if you look deep within yourself. <u>Cadence is defined as a rhythmic flow of sound or words. It is the beat, rate, or measure of any rhythmic movement. Cadence also speaks towards the flow or rhythm of events, especially the pattern in which something is experienced</u>.

What is your cadence? What is your beat? What is your rhythm? If you are having an issue with identifying your cadence, your beat, and your rhythm, you are not alone. Many of us go through life, particularly as adults with a lost cadence, beats, and rhythms. Much of this is because as adults we get so busy trying to make a living that we lose our cadence, beat, and rhythm, which is an important part of living the type of life we are created to live.

A good example of cadence is children, who have the tendency to break into some dance mode without any music playing except for the music in their souls. I am often amused by our oldest grand-daughter who is at the age of seven at the time of me writing this book. There have been times whether sitting in a restaurant, at the house, or in a store, she will start moving with her own beat and rhythm, with no apology. One day, the beat and the rhythm happen again, and in my curiosity, I asked her why she was dancing? While still moving with her inner beat and rhythm that only she could hear, she simply said, "I feel it. It feels good and it is fun. Come on Popi-D, you can do it too." Not wanting to be outdone by a seven-year-old, I got up and attempted to move according to a beat and rhythm that I did not hear. Well, you can imagine what that looked like, trying to keep up with a seven-year-old, who is usually on ten most of the day. So, not wanting to be outdone by a seven-year-old by not taking her challenge, I decided to not try and get into her head to figure out what her beat and rhythm were. So, I decided to simply dance in "Popi-D" style, according to my own beat and rhythm. This made the experience more rewarding.

Other examples of the power of cadence and how it helps us stay the path of our Life Compass are people like Martin Luther King, Eleanor Roosevelt, Malcolm X, Michael Jackson, Tyler Perry, Bill Gates, Bob Marley, Marie Callender, Chris Gardner, Tupac, Biggie Smalls, and Jesus. If we follow their path, we will discover that they live and have lived according to their cadence. They did not allow the circumstances they faced to dictate their rhythm.

If we are honest, we can admit that as adults we often go through life attempting to move by someone else's beat and rhythm, or by the beat and rhythm of what we consider as societal norms. This is sometimes at the expense of us not living according to our own beat, or rhythm – our cadence. When we lose our cadence, we lose our beat and rhythm, and life can go in any direction, versus it going according to our Life Compass.

As it relates to patterning our lives according to our Life Compass and staying aimed in the direction of our True North, cadence plays a major role. It is what helps us get to who we are created to be, as well as leading us to the power and potential that exist within that helps us compose our lives to the Creator's plan for us.

Cadence can be viewed and received as either negative or positive. It is viewed and received negatively when we solely view the rough events in our lives as harm and depletion, versus viewing these rough events as encounters that push us down the path of our compass that leads to our True North.

Cadence can be positive and empowering when we resolve to be intentional about catching our own beat and rhythm and dance our lives accordingly. This can mean breaking away from some societal norms, as well as not being popular in the sight of others. Let us face the fact, that when we live according to our own beat and rhythm, we are sometimes considered as rule breakers.

As we make an honest attempt to live according to our compass and keep our focus on what we are created for and to accomplish, cadence calls for us to develop the courage to go beyond average. I must admit that trying to stay on beat and keep our rhythm, while trying to stay courageous on the path of our compass is not an easy task. But it is a task that can be accomplished with intention, commitment, and persistence.

When it comes to knowing your cadence while following your Life Compass, there are three things that play important roles. I call these the 3-I's of Cadence which are, *Instinct*, *Intuition*, and *Insight*. All of which are closely connected.

INSTINCT: Each of us have instincts. It is an inborn pattern or tendency to actions common to us. It is our natural aptitude of giftedness, that if paid attention to, can make life work for us and enable us to produce the life we envision, as we follow our compass. Living by instinct is as natural as a bee flying from flower to flower and producing honey. The bee moves from flower to flower in sync with its internal rhythm. It is unfortunate, that many of us pay less or no attention to our instincts which can cause us to get out of sync with our cadence. As a result, we can venture off our compass. If we are going to remain on the path of our Life Compass, and get to our True North, it is important that we trust our instinct.

INTUITION: Each of us is born with intuition. It is an innate awareness of something without having actual evidence. It is not necessarily something we develop, versus something that comes from a higher source. Intuition alerts us to what is or isn't for our benefit.

Intuition is that feeling in your gut when you instinctively know that something you are doing or about to do is right or wrong. It is also that feeling in your gut that informs you that you are going in the wrong or right direction.

When it comes to life compassing, your intuition is important to know your cadence. It helps you stay on beat and in rhythm with your Life Compass because it helps you identify what, as well as who, is or isn't beneficial for you as you move in the direction and closer to your True North. As the old saying goes, "Trust your gut."

INSIGHT: When it comes to following your Life Compass to get to your True North, having insight is important as you move with your cadence. Insight is having a sort of x-ray vision to apprehend the true nature of a thing or an event that takes place while you are on your compass path, especially through intuitive understanding.

Living compass driven and knowing your purpose, destiny, and cadence does not exempt you from experiencing events that can cause you to question whether you are on the right path.

Having insight as you move according to your rhythm and beat, as you follow your compass helps you to see the truth of a matter. For example, as you follow your compass path and encounter something that may not be in your favor, through insight you can discover that what seems to be a setback is really a setup, that triggers you to trust your instinct, and abilities, and to stretch your faith to get to the destiny you are born for.

Knowing Your Purpose

Knowing our cadence helps us embrace our purpose. Why do you get out of bed each morning? Are you merely existing, making ends meet, or are you living with purpose? Knowing why you get out of bed each morning is as important as rain and sunshine are to a wildflower. Without the rain and sunshine, the flower will begin to wither and die at some point. So, it is with the essence of our lives. Without knowing our purpose, at some point, we will begin to wither and eventually die, even while we are still alive and going about our daily routines. To wither is to cease to flourish. To fall into some type of decay or decline instead of growing and flourishing. Dying is not always physical. As it relates to not knowing our purpose. To die is to be without liveliness or the spirit to live life at its best. It is to become dull and colorless. We can never live the type of life we envision and desire to really live without us knowing our purpose and living within it.

Our purpose is the reason we exist. You are not on this earth by accident. You are not an afterthought. You were deliberately created by the Creator to do something on this earth that only

106

<u>you can do</u>. Nothing outside of our purpose should give us our reason for existence. They should be an extension of our existence, whether family, careers, jobs, possessions, money, positions, popularity, etc.

When you find out what your purpose of existence is, in most cases, you start pursuing it even if you are wrong and you believe that you are correct, you will not let anybody or anything stand in your way and keep you from living within the realm of your purpose. You are the only person that can keep you from living according to your purpose. Circumstances and others can create obstacles, but if you are determined to reach your purpose no one or nothing can keep you from reaching it.

Life can never be worth living without purpose. Without purpose, we simply exist without ever really living. Without purpose, we wake up each morning meandering through life but not living to our fullest. Purpose helps us live and it gives us a reason for living, even if we must do it alone. If we have no idea as to what our purpose is, it is difficult to arrive at the destiny for which we are created.

Coming to know your purpose, embracing, and living it is one of the best things we can ever discover and do. However, we must understand that it is not without the possibilities of risk and losses.

The day that I started living with purpose, was the day that I really started getting out of bed and wanting to live my best life. Therefore, I put everything on the line to live according to my purpose. Life became exciting. However, I did not calculate that living out my purpose involved risk and losses. I came to realize that while I was pursuing my purpose that many of the people who I thought were my friends, and really loved me, started to abandon me because they deemed me to be confused about my life when I was only embracing and living out my purpose. This did not fit the mold of what society calls normal or what they thought my purpose should be. We must accept the fact that not everyone, even some of the people in our immediate circle will agree with our purpose or support it. This is alright because our purpose is not about what others believe about us but, it is about what we know and believe about ourselves.

When it comes to life compassing, here are some benefits that can be gained when we know and embrace our purpose and begin living it out:

It provides us with a clearer perspective on life. When we know our purpose, we get a sense as to why we get up each day. We become more laser-focused on the path we should be taking throughout the day to accomplish our immediate goals and we waste less time on trivial matters and on the things that are not essential.

It helps us stay more focused on the most meaningful things. We all Have the tendency to waste time addressing things that have no meaning to us. Just because something means something to someone else, does not mean it matters to us. Everything that comes our way does not necessarily have meaning to us. Everything laid before us does not always bring meaning. Some things are not significant because they do not have value to us, and do not assist us in getting to our destiny. If something does not add to us or help us evolve into the person we are created to be, or help us become a better person, or get closer to our destiny, it has no real meaning to us, and we should not entertain it to the point that it depletes our time and energy.

It helps us live longer and healthier. When it comes to living longer and healthier, studies have shown that older adults seem to live longer and healthier than those who have no purpose. They have also shown that people who suffer with terminal illnesses who have purpose, seem to cope better during their ailment than those who have no purpose. In addition, people who have a sense of purpose usually develop healthier habits, and healthier routines. Such as eating healthier, exercising, and proper rest and relaxation, than those who have no sense of their purpose, because they understand the importance of a healthy body that helps them live out their purpose.

It helps us keep our integrity. One of the definitions of integrity is being in a state of being whole, entire, or undiminished. Those who know or have a sense of their purpose are clearer about who they are, and what they are on this earth for. They aim at living their lives according to their core values. They live with genuine passion and not a façade to impress people because they embrace their wholeness. Whenever they show up in any situation or occasion, they show up as their true self and not a knock-off of themselves or someone else.

AFFIRMATION #3

I confirm that I am who and what the Creator says I am, and who and what I perceive myself to be. I am not defined by the perception of others or by the circumstances I encounter. I am talented, gifted, and empowered to live out my "Now" to my fullest potential.

Part 3

Accepting Where You Are, and Owning It

One of the most powerful and revolutionizing things we can ever do to change the course of our lives is acknowledging the season we are in. Like natural seasons, our life changes. These seasonal shifts must be acknowledged if we are going to live our lives to its fullest. Accepting where we are in life is not just about accepting our flaws and weaknesses, it is also about embracing our present strengths, uniqueness and celebrating who we have grown to become without shame or apology.

Chapter 9
Self-Clarity

"The more you know yourself, the more clarity there is. Self-knowing has no end – you don't come to an achievement; you don't come to a conclusion. It is an endless river."
                                                    -Jiddu Krishnamuti

Who are you? Self-Clarity is about who we have evolved into. It is about knowing who you are in the present, and about who you want to be in the future. Self-Clarity suggests that some individuals possess a clear sense of who they are and a sense of where they are going or desire to go in life. Those who have a sense of Self-Clarity are usually aware of their strengths, as well as their weaknesses, the nature of their personalities, and even their attitude about certain issues and values. Whereas those who are void of Self-Clarity are opposite. Self-Clarity refers to people with a clear Self-Concept of who they are.

Self-Clarity is from Self-Esteem. Self-Esteem is considered as an overall evaluation of the self as bad or good. It has much to do with how we see our worth and value. On the other hand, Self-Clarity is about embracing who we are created to be without taking into consideration what others think about us or their perspective of us. Self-Clarity is about taking self-inventory of who we are – the good and the bad and owning it as part of our truth. It plays a major role in how we approach living according to our Life Compass as we take the path that leads to our True North.

I thought the older I became, would lessen the need to be clear about myself and who I had evolved into. I held tightly to this notion, that because I had made it a point to be clear about who I was throughout my younger years. Considering that I have indulged in several careers that I could not have indulged in without being clear of who I was and what I really wanted to do in life. I had worked hard to make sure that I knew myself and what I wanted out of life.

Therefore, the older I became, I suppressed the need for Self-Clarity. I was never taught that Self-Clarity is a continual part of life, particularly for those who are lifetime learners and dreamers. I was just taught to learn as much as I could and keep dreaming and things will turn out for the good eventually. I figured that because I knew what I wanted out of life I would always be clear about who I was. But I came to the realization that because I knew what I wanted out of life at a younger age, did not necessarily mean that I was clear about myself or who I was evolving into as I become older.

Because we are good at doing something does not necessarily mean that we have a clear perspective and picture of who we really are. It could simply mean that we have learned enough about a certain thing, or a certain area and we simply applied what we have learned and begin making it work for us materially. But underneath the surface, there is a missing piece. And that missing piece is clarity concerning who we have really evolved into and what our passions had become. As a result, we can stay in careers and on paths that were based upon who we were once upon a time, but that time changed, and we changed with it sometimes without a clue. As a result, we become a bit confused about who is the person we view in the mirror each morning. When I arrived at this point in my journey, I realized that a part of me had begun to settle for simply making a living, but not really living. There is a difference between making a living and really living. For me, making a living is getting enough training and collecting enough data and sharpening certain skillsets, and plugging it into a certain career field. Living on the other hand is about living the type of life we are created to live and be happy with it. It is living our lives with essence. We can never live our lives in their essence until we are clear about who we have evolved into. Living according to our Life Compass and going in the direction of our True North, requires Self-Clarity. Self-Clarity leads to Authenticity.

Embrace Your Authenticity

Living according to our life Compass and going for our True North is not just about going in a particular direction and down particular paths. It is also about who we are as we go in these directions and take these paths. It is also about embracing who we are, as well as who we are evolving into becoming as we put forth honest efforts to live compass driven.

I have discovered that as one takes the path of their Life Compass and stays focused on their True North, it is important that we come to grips with who we are authentically. As the old saying goes, "to thou self be true." We can never be true to ourselves, or to the path of our Life Compass when we fail to embrace who we are and who we are evolving into becoming. And we will never arrive at our True North while pushing our authenticity to the side, perhaps hoping to become something or someone we are not created to be.

As it relates to living compass driven, I define Authenticity as, not being false or a copy of someone else or something else. It is remaining who we are created to be as we evolve on our path. It is being the same person regardless of what we encounter on our path. As I make an honest attempt to follow my own compass, one of the temptations I am sometimes faced with, and maybe you can relate. And that temptation is, to put our true self in a box hidden from the world. Sometimes this is because it is our nature to devalue what we can offer the world at times. Then there are times when we become a knock-off of ourselves due to fear of rejection by others because we are not for sure if our original self will be received or valued by others. Such beliefs concerning ourselves can easily knock us off our compass. And we get lost in the hustles, and bustle of trying to be someone other than who we are created to be.

We can never find our Life Compass or remain on its path or reach our True North, until we accept who we are – flaws and all. If we live as knockoffs and copies of who we are versus originals, we will never step into our authentic flow that will eventually lead us to our destiny. When we reject or ignore our real selves, we cheapen who we are as awesome creations of God. And we are not created cheaply. I love the Scriptural rendering in Psalm 139:14 that says, *"...I am fearfully and wonderfully made; your works are wonderful..."* When we fail to grasp an understanding of how wonderfully we are created, we devalue who we are and overlook our worth beyond what we have accumulated materially.

Knowing and accepting who we are authentically is empowering because it empowers us to live according to our Life Compass and stay determined to reach our True North.

Embracing our authenticity is important as we take the path of our Life Compass and find our True North, because our Life Compass and our True North match our personality traits, potential, abilities, giftedness, and attitudes concerning certain events, values, etc. These particularities play major roles in the path of our compass. They are also what we employ to get to our True North – our destiny. When we are not being authentic, we can easily be drawn down paths that are not meant for us, and we risk missing arriving at our destiny.

Don't be a Knockoff – Be the Original You

If one is not careful to live authentically, we can spend our lives living as knockoffs versus originals, like art sold on a street corner that has no real value. Knockoffs can resemble the real thing. If you do not have a clue of what makes an original, you can pay a high cost for something that is not real. I learned this lesson in my early twenties when I purchased what I thought was an original Rolex. I should have known better by the price I paid. But on the other hand, I had no clue about the originality of a real Rolex. To make a long story short, when I decided I wanted to sell what I thought was an original Rolex, I discovered that I had purchased as well as was walking around wearing a fake that had no value. You can imagine the level of my disappointment, as well as my embarrassment.

<u>Some people live as knockoffs versus originals – fake lives, trying to resemble someone or something that they are not created to be, only to discover that when it is time to weigh their true value, what and who they were attempting to be, have no value at all</u>. Being a knockoff of ourselves instead of being originals can be dangerous and costly. It is dangerous and costly, because while we are being knockoffs and not originals we fail at the following:

We fail to embrace who we really are, and we lose our truest selves in the process. We will never get to who are and where we are purposed to be in life if we are not living authentically.

We fail to understand our truest value. Each of us regardless of our station in life has value, whether we recognize it or not. The only way we can know our truest value is by living as originals.

We fail to enter and live in the domain for which we are created. There is a domain in which we fit. When we live in the domain we are created for, everything and every blessing meant for us is released into our lives.

We fail to utilize our giftedness that makes life more enjoyable. We will always overlook our capabilities when we live as knock-offs and not originals. While being knockoffs and not originals, we spend much of our time emulating others, while failing to live according to our potential, which makes life less enjoyable.

One of the most rewarding and empowering things we can do for ourselves as we attempt to live according to our Life Compass and find our True North, that is to "Knockoff being a knockoff" and get back to being an original.

Change Your Impossible to I'm-Possible

As we accept where we are and own it, acknowledge our Life Compass, and go in the direction of our True North, it is imperative that we are intentional about changing our "Impossible" to "I'm-Possible." I'm-Possible" is about acknowledging what we are capable of accomplishing once we put our minds towards it, and applying our abilities, potential, talents, giftedness, mental powers, and spiritual empowerment. It is about unleashing our inner possibilities. Each of us is filled with awesome possibilities that can change the course of our lives for the better. Unfortunately, many people go through life not realizing that they are filled with great possibilities. As a result, they miss what life has to offer them, or they settle for just a portion of what life has to offer them, and their possibilities go untapped and unreleased. When we fail to acknowledge and release our possibilities, we do not only cheat ourselves, but we also cheat the world, because our possibilities are not just to be used for our own benefit, but also for the benefit of others. Each of us has been uniquely created to do something that can help change ourselves and the world for the better, whether that something is large or small. But to do this we must have the courage and faith to change our Impossible to I'm-Possible.

We will never get on the path we are supposed to be on if we do not believe that we are filled with positive possibilities regardless of our situations and circumstances. I know this all too well in my journey. I spent most of my life looking through the lens of what I considered impossible instead of what was possible. However, I concluded that if my life was going to be what it was designed to be, and if I was going to live according to my Life Compass and find my True North, I had to muster up the courage to challenge my impossibilities by starting to embrace the power of I'm-Possible. See, there is power in "I'm-Possible." When we tap into the power of "I'm-Possible" it helps us to realize that there is power in us that can change the course of lives despite our past and present condition of existence.

To tap into these possibilities and release them, it starts with us looking deeply within ourselves. Possibilities are not just in the world they are in us. We are born with them.

Changing our "Impossible" to "I'm-Possible" does not occur by happenstance or by some surge of luck. It occurs when we tap into our inner selves and discover or rediscover the possibilities that are already in us and release them. When we do this, we begin to chart our lives by what is possible as we face ourselves each day, we can declare that "I'm-Possible." To live in the power of "I'm-Possible," I suggest several things that I contend will help compass our lives by what is possible for us:

Don't allow your past regardless of how far back or recent it is to dictate or determine your present and future possibilities. Remember that because you failed at accomplishing something in the past does not mean you cannot accomplish it in the present. There are times when we set out to accomplish something, but the season is not ripe for it. All good fruit has a season.

Trust your own instinct of your possibilities. If you believe something is possible and that it can be accomplished, go for it. Do not allow what others believe or perceive to be impossible, persuade you to doubt what you know is possible. Stick to your beliefs.

Practice convincing yourself that what you aim to accomplish is possible. The first person you need to convince as it relates to your possibilities is you. Everyone else's opinion is secondary. If you are not convinced of what is possible for you, it does not matter what others believe. So, practice convincing yourself of your possibilities through positive self-Affirmations.

Stay connected to the source of your possibilities. For me, God is my source of all possibilities. For you, your source of all possibilities may be otherwise. But whatever your source of possibilities is, stay connected.

Changing Your "What If?"

To get on the course of your Life Compass and maintain the path and stay focused on what you believe is your True North and change your "Impossible" to "I'm Possible" it is important that you change your "What if?"

We usually use the phrase "What if" negatively.

What if it doesn't work?
What if I can't afford it?
What if I'm not good enough?
What if I can't break the habit?
What if they leave me?
What if I change careers and I fail?
What if I be me and they don't accept me?
What if I don't get the job?
What if I don't lose the weight?

The list goes on. These are limiting perspectives that keep you from embracing the manifestation of the possibilities of you living a fulfilled life. They cause you to abandon your possibilities. But what if you start using "What if?" in a positive manner?

What if I try something new or different and it works?
What if I start the business and it grows?
What if I stop limiting myself?
What if I stop being a victim and start living victoriously?
What if I break the habit?

What if I stop being angry and start living a happy life?
What if I just start being me?
What if I let go of my negative past?
What if I get over my past mistakes?
What if I lose weight?

The list goes on. If you start using your "What if?" in a positive way, you can change the direction your life goes, and it flows into a vast ocean full of wonderful things that will empower you to live a fulfilled life without limits according to your Life Compass, as well as the life you have been designed to live and enjoy.

Chapter 10
Life-Detoxification

"Today I will detox my mind, body and life. I will renew it with good, clean, powerful and positive."

-Billy Cox

P art of the process of living by our Life Compass and getting to our True North is practicing detoxing our lives as we go. Usually when we think of the term "detoxification," we lean towards the idea or process of ridding ourselves of some substance that affects our minds or body. Detoxing is a process by which toxins are changed into being less toxic or more excretable substances. **"Life-Detoxification" leans towards the idea and process of ridding ourselves of the various toxins we have developed over time, which sometimes go un-noticed that affects how we live our lives, as well as how we deal with the various circumstances we encounter in life**. Such as patterns of thinking, and habits that we have accumulated over time.

There are times in each person's life when we are affected by the various events and people we encounter. All the events and people we encounter are not negative. But some are, and we must identify them, as well as release them to follow our Life Compass and get to our True North. Because we encounter negative events that sometimes involve people, there comes a time that we must detox ourselves of them. This is not always an easy task to perform. But it must be done if we are going to follow the path of our compass and arrive at our destiny.

In addition, there comes a time when we must rid ourselves of "Self-Toxins" that has been developed by one-self. "Self-Toxins" can be described in my opinion as unhealthy habits, certain beliefs, or a school of thoughts developed over time that prohibits us from moving forward in a positive and healthy way. In addition, it can also be described as the words, idioms, and expressions we sometimes use to define and describe our life journey. I am a firm believer in the power of our words. When negatives words, idioms, and expressions are used to describe our journey, or how we see the world, others, and ourselves, they sometimes become manifested in our condition of existence, and we can become affected by the toxins thereof. Proverbs 18:21 says, *"The tongue has the power of life and death, and those who love it will eat its fruit."* Therefore, as it relates to life detoxification, it is imperative that we watch what we speak into our atmosphere.

Because each of us is sometimes subject and vulnerable to various toxic variables that are present in life, whether noticed or not, it becomes necessary for us to take the time and engage in what I term as a "Life-Detoxification" process that will help us follow our Life Compass and get to our True North.

Anyone can detox if they make up their minds to do so. Again, detoxing is a process that simply takes time, discipline, determination along with faith and confidence. In Life compassing and going for our destiny, Life-Detoxification is not a one-time process, it becomes a way one chooses to live their life.

Mental Maintenance

Part of Life-Detoxification is mental maintenance. For example, part of getting our vehicles serviced regularly is to get old fluids replaced with fresh fluids, as well as to make sure that things are well for extra miles. When it comes to Life-Detoxification, mental maintenance helps us identify certain thoughts, thinking patterns, and beliefs that are no longer healthy for our present life journey. This is not to imply that the thoughts, thinking patterns, and beliefs did not work for us. However, there are times when the thoughts, thinking patterns, and beliefs that worked for us do not fit the path we are presently on. We must come to grips with the fact that some of the thoughts, thinking patterns, and beliefs we have may not lead us to the new life we desire. Therefore, it calls for mental maintenance. Mental maintenance can be considered as simply bringing our thoughts, thinking patterns, and beliefs up to date to fit the path we are currently on that matches our Life Compass.

The mind is the strongest muscle in the human body, as well as the most important. In my opinion. I also believe our minds and the condition of our minds plays a vital role as we follow the path of our compass as we shoot for our destiny.

Mental Maintenance is imperative. I came to grips with the importance of mental maintenance later in my life. I knew that the condition of my mind was important as it pertained to me getting to where I wanted to go. However, I did not look at it from a perspective of maintenance. Perhaps I thought that my mind would be healthy if I engaged in learning events and read more books. I discovered that even though I was attending conferences and speaking at conferences, I was missing engaging in mental maintenance. Therefore, even though I was engaging in what I term as mind building events, I was not engaging in processes that help me maintain my mental health. As I think about it, I did not engage in mental health processes, because I viewed mental health or maintenance as something persons who were dealing with some type of mental illnesses needed. I later discovered that regardless of who we are, and our station or position in life, it is important that we engage in mental maintenance.

Maintenance, in my opinion, is not necessarily about fixing something, versus it being about maintaining the health of something or adding to it for the sake of its health.

When it comes to life compassing and staying focused in the direction of our True North, we must practice mental maintenance because the condition of our minds, as well as what is in our minds sometimes determine how we operate on our compass path, as well as how focused we remain on the direction of our True North.

There are four steps that can lead to Mental Maintenance:

Step One: Take the time to take inventory of your thoughts, thinking patterns, and beliefs that you are loyal to. During this portion of the process, you will have to take into consideration where these thoughts, thinking patterns, and beliefs come from. Some of our thoughts, thinking patterns, and beliefs are handed down from generations that may not fit us currently.

Step Two: Make a list of thoughts, thinking patterns, and beliefs that do not fit where you are presently. This takes honesty and courage. It takes honesty because it calls for us to admit that we are no longer where we used to be in our journey. It takes courage because it sometimes means that we will have to break rank with the herds we are accustomed to.

Step Three: Make a list of the thoughts, thinking patterns, and beliefs that will help you become productive as you take the path of your life compass.

Step Four: Compose a list of things (strategies) you can employ to replace your outdated thoughts, thinking patterns, and beliefs that will help you stick to the path of your compass and stay on the path that leads to your True North.

Necessary Endings

Another part of Detoxification is knowing when to end some things. Life compassing and finding our True North, is not just about what we start, it is also about what we decide to end. In life compassing and finding our True North it is important that we arrive at a place in our journey when we recognized it is necessary to end some things. Dr. Henry Cloud says in his book entitled, "Necessary Ending," "Today may be the enemy of your tomorrow. In your business and perhaps your life, the tomorrow that you desire and envision may never come to pass if you do not end some things, you are doing today. For some people, that is clear and easy to execute. They end the things that are holding them back. For others, it is more difficult." Whether it is easy or difficult, if we are going to live according to the path of our Life Compass and eventually find our True North, we must identify those things in our lives that are holding us back from seeing and embracing the good life we envision. If we take a close look at Ecclesiastes 3:1-8 (NIV), we will discover that ending things plays a prevalent role in our lives as we attempt to follow our compass path and shoot for our destiny.

"There is a time for everything, and a season for every activity under heaven: a time to be born and a time to die, a time to plant and a time to uproot, a time to kill and a time to heal, a time to tear down and a time to build, a time to weep and a time to laugh, a time to mourn and a time to dance, a time to scatter stones and a time to gather them, a time to embrace and a time to refrain, a time to search and a time to give up, a time to keep and a time to throw away, a time to tear and a time to mend, a time to be silent and a time to speak, a time to love and a time to hate, a time for war and time for peace." – **Ecclesiastes 3:1-8 (NIV)**

Everything has a season, and we must identify and embrace our current season that helps us to thrive in every area of our lives as we follow the path of our compass. As we welcome our season, we must also welcome endings. As it relates to life compassing, ending something is not just about ending those things that we deem as negative that prohibits us from moving to higher levels, it is also about possibly ending some things that worked for us in our previous season of our journey. When I started to make an honest attempt to do this, I arrived at the shocking reality that I had to be willing to let go of some things that once worked for me. Our tendency is to try to duplicate past accomplishments and methodologies that worked well in our last season. I realized that the season I had entered and who I had evolved into required something different. Some of my frustrations that came as I was attempting to align myself according to my compass, was that I wanted to relive my best past. Do not get me wrong. There is nothing wrong with longing for the best of our lives to be part of our present. However, there are times when the best of our past does not fit into the scheme of things in our present. As we live according to our Life

Compass, there will be times when we must be innovative and take the things that once worked and reshape them to fit our present journey.

Necessary endings in life compassing are also about us determining what relationships with others that we need to let go of so we can move forward in a healthy manner. This is difficult to do at times. For some people, this is an easy task to perform. For others, it is a major task that is full of emotions, even when we know without a doubt that some of the people, we are connected to are not good for us, and have kept us from really living life at its best possible. It is difficult to end some relationships, particularly if you live by the seat of your heart and emotions. One of the most difficult things I had to do when I decided to really make an honest attempt to follow my compass, was to come to grips with the reality that I had to detach myself from some of the people that I was intricately connected to because I came to the reality that some were toxic. Toxic people never encourage us to follow our compass. Instead, they usually detour us off the path of our compass.

Another aspect of necessary endings is ending a certain relationship that exists within ourselves. Hmm? I contend that each person has a personality – another person within us that can keep us from moving forward in various capacities. We must recognize this personality and the inner person with whom we have a relationship, and say to that portion of us, "You can't reside in me anymore." If not, we will continue to feed and nurture this personality and person and feed the relationship that keeps us where we are and prevent us from moving forward. Some things must come to an end, even if it is a portion of ourselves. I discovered that sometimes it is not others or other things that stand in our way and keep us from progressing. Many times, we stand in our own way. We must get out of the way of ourselves by releasing the best of who we are and letting go of that portion of ourselves that no longer works if we are going to live a compass driven life that leads to our destiny.

No Apologies Needed

I have discovered that even though detoxing our lives to follow the path of our Life Compass is necessary, we must be intentional about ending some things, it is not always easy. For me, it is difficult because it sometimes causes me to feel somewhat guilty for ridding myself of some things and some people, and I feel the need to apologize for the changes I have made and are trying to make. But I later concluded, that if I am going to live according to my Life Compass and stay true to my True North, I had to get past the need of apologizing for making the right changes in my life.

I was taught never to be selfish. As a result, I always put others before me, which often depleted me of what I needed to live. Even to the point that I put forth much effort helping people find their compass, as well as inspired them to go for their destiny without apologizing to anyone for deciding to live their best life possible. While I was encouraging them, I was failing to encourage myself. I did this because of my view of selfishness. I was never taught that there is a portion of selfishness that is required if one is to follow their Life Compass and find their True North. I call this a "Righteous-Selfishness." I define a "Righteous-Selfishness" as having the right to do for ourselves what is needed to get to the type of life we are created to live, as well as having the right to maintain our path that leads to our destiny. Without it, we will give away the best of ourselves and have nothing more to give and nothing for ourselves. I ran across the following story on Facebook by Joe Hansley concerning a homeless man he met that speaks towards the idea of "Righteous-Selfishness":

"I seen a homeless guy at Popeyes in Memphis and I gave him some loose ones in my pocket…and he said "thank you"…so I asked him…"how did you get to this point?"… he looked up, smiled and said "SHOWING LOVE" …I asked… "what do you mean?"…he said I went thru my whole life making sure everyone else was ok no matter what was going right or wrong in my life I did for others…I never wanted to see others go without…I asked "do you regret it?"…he said no it just hurt me to my soul that the very people I gave the shirt off my back to…wouldn't give me a sleeve off that same shirt when I was in need…he said…its better to build your house and invite someone in for shelter…then to hand them your bricks while you building yours…cause if you keep handing them bricks from the house that you supposed to be building for you… you will turn around 1 day and that spot where you have planned to build your house will be a empty lot…then you are the one that's looking for bricks."

A "Righteous-Selfishness" is not about withholding from others. It is about keeping a portion of ourselves for ourselves so, that we will have something to give to others. If we give everything away, we become depleted of what is needed for our journey, and we have nothing to offer others we meet on the journey. When there is not a sense of "Righteous-Selfishness, we tend to have the urge to apologize for the changes we make to make our lives better and follow our compass path and go for our destiny.

There are times when an apology is in order and necessary, particularly when we have offended someone or have caused someone pain or harm in some form or another. On the other hand, there are some things we should never apologize for. Here are seven things you should never apologize for as you live according to your Life Compass and find your True North.

Never apologize for being your authentic self. You are created uniquely. Live your uniqueness out loud and in the light for the world to see. The universe rewards uniqueness and not duplicates.

Never apologize for taking risks for what you desire out of life, no matter who disagrees. It is your life, and you should live it according to your own compass, even if you must go at it alone.

Never apologize for breaking toxic relationships, no matter who it is with. Toxic people are draining and eroding. Maybe they are not for you at this time in your life. When we remain in toxic relationships, we become toxic over time.

Never apologize for saying "No" when needed. Many people take on too much to satisfy others while draining themselves. You cannot get to the "Yes's" that life has to offer you if you never say "No" to some things and to some people.

Never apologize for carving out time for yourself. Making time for yourself is essential for a happy and giving life. We cannot pour into others from an empty vessel.

Never apologize for your imperfections. No one is perfect. Those who really love us accept us for who we truly are and help us to become better and grow to be better without diminishing us.

Never apologize for loving yourself. We can love ourselves without being conceited and selfish. The first step towards loving others is to first love yourself. We cannot give what we do not have.

Release the Weights!

Part of Detoxification is releasing the weights that hold us down. As a certified scuba diver, one of the most important lessons and arts we were taught in case we find ourselves underwater and running out of oxygen, is how to release the weights. Let me explain. The scuba vest consists of air and weights, not including the oxygen tank we carry. The air in the vest is managed along with weights to give the diver even buoyancy while underwater, which allows them to level off while underwater. The oxygen in the scuba tank is only for breathing while underwater. The amount of oxygen in the tank is managed by a timer that tells the diver how long they can remain underwater. Unfortunately, there are times when the diver fails to pay close attention to the timer, or the tank can malfunction. In the case of either, this can cause a serious issue for the diver, particularly if they are at forty to fifty feet underwater. The good news is that even if the tank malfunctions or run out of oxygen, there's still air in the scuba vest that if managed properly can be enough to get the diver to the surface. The bad news is that it becomes almost impossible to float to the surface with limited air while continuing to carry the weights in the pockets of the scuba vest. The good news is that the weights can be released at any time during the ordeal, by simply pulling a cord connected to each pocket of the vest that contains a weight. When the cord is pulled, all the weights are released at the same time, which allows the diver to ascend to the surface.

There are times when we find ourselves at some depth in life that threatens to take our breath away and we begin to drown.

Particularly when we fail to release the weights that are keeping us under. At some point we all carry weight, whether the weight is placed upon us by ourselves, others, or life circumstances. Regardless of the source or sources of the weight, the impact it has on us can change if we remember that in many cases, we have the choice to carry the weights placed on us or we can release them.

It is not always easy to release the weights we carry that keep us from rising to the top of things because we can become accustomed to carrying the weights, even though they are heavy, and we rather not carry them. After all, we may have been carrying them for a long time, and carrying them has become second nature, even while we are suffocating and being depleted with what we need to live the type of life we desire. Regardless of how deep we are in some places in life, we can rise to the top and live according to our Life Compass and get to our True North, if we are intentional and determined to drop unnecessary weight.

As we are set out to live compass driven and move in the direction of our destiny, I suggest the following as it pertains to releasing the weights during our journey.

+ *Acknowledge when you are being weighed down and depleted of the oxygen you need to live your best life. Pretending that they do not exist will not make the weight lighter.*
+ *Identify the source of the weight you are carrying, even if it is you. Weight does not just appear. It comes from somewhere and is caused by something.*
+ *Resolve that you no longer want to carry the weight. If you do not conclude that you no longer want something, it will remain.*
+ *Be intentional and determined to drop the weights you have been carrying. Weights do not go away on their own.*

✦ *Rely on your source of power to release the weights you have been carrying and have the faith that your source of power is present to help you release the weights.*

Chapter 11

Self-Inventory

Knowing yourself has to always come from within. The out-side can inspire or guide you, but knowing has to come from within you."

-Jaggi Vasudev

To eventually get to where we are created to be, we must be open to accepting where we are presently in our journey, as well as being open to accepting the person we have evolved into. This requires Self-Inventory in several areas of our lives. Conducting an inventory of ourselves can be somewhat scary. But it can also be surprising, as well as empowering.

Self-Inventory can be scary in the sense that we may discover that some of the things that we thought no longer existed in us are still present, but they have been lying dormant. This is alright because if they are awakened, and we know what they are, we can subdue them and keep them under control as we maneuver the path of our compass.

Self-Inventory can be surprising because, sometimes during the process we discover some unique and awesome things about ourselves that we had no clue existed, such as new desires, new dislikes, untapped skill sets, and abilities along with new beliefs, as well as fresh views of the world and others.

Self-Inventory can be empowering in the sense that while we are taking the path of our Life Compass, we know what we are working with which can help us reach our True North. I contend that when we have no clue of the things that make us who we are, it is impossible to live the life we desire to live and are capable of living.

Engaging in Self-Inventory helps us identify the things that exist in our lives that often determine how we operate on our compass, as we attempt to keep the path that leads to our destiny. Self-Inventory is about taking a close look at ourselves as it pertains to our strengths and weaknesses, as well as our triggers and drivers. These can be negative or positive. Whether they are negative or positive, they must be identified to live our best life possible. Self-Inventory involves other aspects of inventory, such as Life-Inventory, Spiritual-Inventory, Mental-Inventory, Physical-Inventory, and Emotional-Inventory. When we engage in these types of inventories, we come to know ourselves better. When we get a clearer perspective of ourselves, we have a better chance of knowing what we want and what we do not want, and why.

Life-Inventory

Life-Inventory is about taking a close look at the aspects of our life, to get a clear picture of where we are and who we have evolved into by taking into consideration the experiences of our past. Whether those experiences were negative or positive. Life-Inventory is about taking the time to identify our characteristics and temperament in various categories of our life as it relates to our experiences.

When we do Life-Inventory we reflect on the various events, experiences, pains, celebrations, failures, successes, etc. that have taken place in our lives, and we link them together to get a bigger picture of how we arrived at the point we are presently, and how they can fit together for our best future. When we do Life-Inventory it helps us connect the dots. In other words, it helps us see how the various events of our past, whether they were negative or positive, connect and play a role in getting us to where we are and who we are. For me, the various events of my past as helped me get a clearer perspective of who I have evolved into, as well as inform my values and expectations.

To do a Life-Inventory, take the time to do the following:

+ Get a bird's-eye view of your past. Remember that you are not going back to your past, you are only reviewing your past. This can be a bit painful depending on your approach. I'll say more about this in Chapter twelve.

+ Take the time to identify how the experiences of your past connect to each other in getting you to where you are. You will discover that every experience played a role in your life development. Depending on how we use our past experiences, we will either be stronger or weaker, or bitter or better.

+ Take the time to identify lessons you have learned from your past that will help you be the awesome and unique person who you are created to be.

+ Take the time to compose your life goals, such as a plan to travel more, take on a new career, or ways to promote more happiness in your life.

Spiritual-Inventory

We are spiritual beings, whether we acknowledge it or not. We are spiritual beings living in physical bodies. Connecting the two existences and having them work in harmony with each other, can sometimes be a difficult task.

Some people make no distinction between religion and spirituality. From my perspective religion is different from spirituality. I see religion as a set of organized beliefs and practices, that are carried out by persons who belong to a community group. Spirituality on the other hand is more of individual practices that have to do with one having a sense of purpose as one is connected to what and who he believes is his higher source of power. Again, my higher source of power that gives me purpose is God the Creator.

Your source of power that gives you purpose may be something or someone else other than God the Creator. Regardless of who and what we hold to as being our source of power and purpose we are informed by such connection through our spiritual senses.

I have discovered in my relationship with God the Creator, that when I have a solid connection with Him as my personal source of guidance, I am less available to be controlled by others and by my circumstances. I become my own guru as it pertains to how I live the life I am gifted with, as I am guided by my spiritual source.

Since we are spiritual beings and our spiritual connectiveness helps us move according to our path, it is imperative that we consider engaging in spiritual inventory.

To do a Spiritual-Inventory, take the time to do the following:

+ Take the time to identify who or what you believe is your higher source of power that informs you of your purpose.

+ Take the time to identify what role your higher spiritual source plays in your life journey.

+ Take the time to identify your spiritual beliefs and values, and how they inform your purpose as you take the path that leads to your destiny.

+ Take the time to set spiritual goals that can draw you closer to your spiritual source.

Mental-Inventory

How we operate in life is often determined by what is in our minds. Our minds are composed of thoughts and beliefs that often determine our perspective of things, people, and encounters, as well as how we respond to them. As it is important that we take inventory of the different things in our lives that possibly help us reorganize and stay on the path leading to our destiny, it is just as important that we take the time to inventory our thoughts, beliefs, and thinking patterns. When we take the time to engage in Mental-Inventory, we can discover that some of the thoughts, beliefs, and thinking patterns to which we have become accustomed, do not match where we are currently in our lives, nor where we say we desire to go.

When we do Mental-Inventory, it helps us cultivate the type of thoughts, beliefs, and thinking patterns that promote living productive lives painted with awesome possibilities, as we weed out those thoughts, beliefs, and thinking patterns that are prohibiting. James Allen in his book, entitled, "As A Man Thinketh" says, "A man's mind may be likened to a garden, which may be intelligently cultivated or allowed to run wild; but whether cultivated or neglected, it must, and will bring forth. If no useful seeds are put into it, then an abundance of useless weed seeds will fall therein

and will continue to produce their kind. Just as a gardener culti-
vates his plot, keeping it free from weeds, and growing the flowers
and fruits, which he requires, so may a man tend the garden of his
mind, weeding out all the wrong, useless, and impure thoughts, and
cultivating toward perfection the flowers and fruit of right, useful,
and pure thoughts."

To do a Mental-Inventory take the time to do the following:

+ Take the time to identify and make a list of your thoughts,
  beliefs, and thinking patterns that may be prohibiting you
  from living your best life.
+ Take the time to identify and make a list of your thoughts,
  beliefs, and thinking patterns that promote your best life.
+ Discover ways you can begin to cultivate positive thoughts,
  beliefs, and thinking patterns that can promote a healthy
  mind.
+ Take the time to compose mental goals that will promote
  a healthier mind.

Physical-Inventory

Our body is a gift and must be treated as such if we are going
to get the best out of it. We should desire that our bodies are as
healthy as possible. It is interesting that many people spend more
time doing maintenance of their automobiles and homes, as well
as other items than they do their bodies. Our body is important
and is intricately connected to our mind and soul. Drew Canole,
the Founder of Fitlife.tv. in his book entitled, "*You Be You*" says,
"Although your body is ultimately just a vessel for your spiritual,
vibrational self, your body, mind, and spirit are so deeply inter-
twined that you can't transform one without the areas shifting to

accommodate the whole you. If all the brilliance of your individual light is going to shine through you and out into the world, the practice of developing a harmonious relationship with your body is imperative. Without this important piece of your transformation, you will be left feeling out of sorts, or "off" instead of feeling light and free, flowing effortlessly through life."

Paying attention to our bodies is one of the most important things we can ever do. Our bodies change over time, and we must be mindful of the changes. As it relates to living our best life possible, we must identify both good and bad habits that we engage in that either help us live longer and better, as well as those habits we engage in that, may prohibit us from living longer and better. I discover more and more as I grow older, how important it is to engage in Physical-Inventory. As the mind is a terrible thing to waste, so is our health. Doing Physical inventory helps us to come to grips with the habits and routines that do not promote good health, as well as discover that we may be doing some healthy things that we are not aware of, that if continued and cultivated can help us become healthier or maintain a good health routine.

To do a Physical-Inventory take the time to do the following:

+ Make a list of the bad habits and routines that you know that do not promote proper health, such as eating too much junk food, overconsumption of alcohol, not eating a balanced meal regularly, not getting enough rest and relaxation, or not exercising on a regular basis or simply not having time for fun activities.
+ Make a list of the healthy habits and routines that you are doing that promote a healthy body and cultivate them.
+ Take the time to plan healthy meals and make the time to enjoy the meal, instead of eating in a rush.

◆ Make the time to compose healthy goals. As it is important for us to compose life goals that usually include careers goals, it is just as important to create healthy physical goals.

Emotional-Inventory

We are emotional beings. Some people are more emotional than others. However, we all tend to operate by our emotions. Operating by our emotions is not all bad if we keep our emotions in check and balance. Our emotional makeup plays a vital role in how we live our lives and how we approach and respond to the various events that take place in our lives.

When we are emotionally unhealthy, we have the tendency to deal with the events and circumstances we encounter in unhealthy ways. When we are emotionally healthy, approach things in healthy ways. If we are to live balanced lives, our emotions must be balanced.

Doing an Emotional-Inventory helps us to determine whether we are emotionally healthy or unhealthy. I have discovered that we can sometimes find ourselves existing and responding between unhealthy emotions and healthy emotions, depending on the circumstance and how mindful we are about our feelings at the time the event occurred.

Much of our emotional response to the negative circumstances we encounter has more to do with us than the circumstances. Dr. David Walton, in his book entitled, *Emotional Intelligence: A Practical Guide* states the following: "Our view of ourselves, our confidence, self-esteem, sense of purpose and awareness of the way we tend to react to things provides the basis for self-management, i.e., the ability to stay flexible and behave in a proper and effective way, appropriate to the situation you are in."

To do an Emotional-Inventory take the time to do the following:

+ Take the time to evaluate who you are emotionally, i.e., how you respond to negative or positive circumstances, etc.

+ Take the time to identify the foundation or causes for your emotional response to certain situations, i.e., up-bringing, past rejection, past losses, past pain or current, disappointments, etc.

+ Take the time to identify what triggers your emotional responses, i.e., positive emotions and negative emotions.

+ Take the time to set emotional goals, i.e., how to respond to negative situations effectively and constructively and how to maintain a positive emotional balance.

Chapter 12

Realigning with Your Compass

"Do not follow where the path may lead. Go instead where there is no path and leave a trail."

-Ralph Waldo Emerson

"Where the way is hardest, there go thou. Follow your own path and let people talk."

-Dante Alighieri

Have you ever driven a vehicle that needed an alignment? I know I have. It made for a not so pleasant ride regardless of the distance I was going. If you have ever driven any form of vehicle that needs an alignment, you notice that it tends to drift to the left and it takes more effort to steer and keep straight. This is not indicating that one does not arrive where they plan to. However, the drive is shaky and a bit more tedious, and not as smooth. Sometimes vehicles get out of alignment because of sudden disturbances or impacts from hitting something such as potholes, bumping into curbs, or by going too fast over speed bumps, or by an accident.

There are times throughout our lives when we experience sudden disturbances or are impacted by some unexpected event, or even hit potholes in our journey, as well as moving too fast over speed bumps when we should be slowing down, or encounter accidents caused by ourselves, others or simply because life happens. When this happens, our lives can fall out of alignment, and we can go through life with being out of line with our Life Compass.

When our lives are off their compass, it can be like an automobile that needs an alignment. It tends to drift to the left, and it takes more effort to steer and keep straight. Because of our humanity, we all need to realign our lives to match our Life Compass.

I know this firsthand. As it relates to being out of alignment with our Life Compass it is not about one not doing things that are deemed as successful. For me, it was not about being successful in the things that I was doing during a certain period in my life. However, it was about me not having the courage to shift gears that would have taken me to new levels. As a result, I became comfortable with the way things were, even though I have the ability and potential to do more and to be more. I was not aligning with my Life Compass. I believe that this caused me to miss some of the best seasons of my life. I pray and hope that this will not be your case.

After coming into the awareness that I was not in alignment with my Life Compass, I resolved to become committed to embracing my compass and realign my life accordingly. I encourage you to make a commitment to yourself to realign yourself with your Life Compass and not continue to drift to the left.

You can know when you are out of alignment with your Life Compass. Here are five indicators that you are out of alignment with your Life Compass:

You Are Uninspired. When you are aligned with your Life Compass, you usually operate within the flow of your purpose. Operating according to our purpose inspires you because you are in alignment with why you exist. When you are out of alignment with your purpose you lose inspiration.

You Take Paths that Don't Match Your Abilities. When you are in alignment with your Life Compass, you take paths that allow you to use your natural abilities, by which you feel fulfilled. When you are out of alignment with your compass, you will more than likely take paths that don't match your natural abilities. As a result, you will usually attempt to do something that you are not created to do. This can be frustrating.

You Continually Feel That Something Is Off. When you are not in alignment with your Life Compass, something feels off. You may not know how to describe it, but you know that something doesn't feel right, and you are not comfortable with it.

You Feel Guilty About What You Are Not doing. When you are out of alignment with your Life Compass, guilt sets in. The guilt comes from your knowing that you can do more than what you are doing and have more to offer to the world than what you are giving, you are cheating yourself out of the life you can live and have envisioned.

You Continually Long for More. When you are out of alignment with your Life Compass there is a void. This void exists because you are not using your giftedness, abilities, and talents, which causes you not to live according to your purpose. When you are not living according to your purpose, you will never be satisfied.

Realignment is about taking the necessary actions of changing or restoring ourselves and lives to a different or its former position or state. It is about putting things back into their proper place, or forming new arrangements and having a new orientation about ourselves, others, and the world. When it comes to life compassing, realignment helps us get on our compass, as well as helps us to maintain proper and healthy balance as we follow the path of our compass that eventually gets us to our True North.

What will happen in your life if you resolve to become committed to getting in alignment or back in alignment with your purpose according to your Life Compass, which puts you in position to eventually reach the awesome destiny you are created and equipped to reach? Let me tell you what will happen. You will begin to live your full best life despite your challenges and not so favorable situations. When we are in alignment with the path we are created for and committed to following it, no sudden disturbance, impact, unexpected event, pothole, or speed bump can keep us from reaching our True North.

Realigning with our Life Compass to get to our True North is important, but it does not just happen because we acknowledge its importance. There are some actions we must take if we are going to realign with our Life Compass. Here are six ways you can align with your Life Compass:

Review Your Life Journey. It is critically important during compassing that we pause occasionally to review where we are in our life journey. It gives us the chance to ask ourselves questions, such as: Where have I arrived? Where am I going? Am I on the right track? Am I there yet? When we pause to entertain these types of questions it helps us know whether we need to realign. There are times when we will discover as we review our life journey that we are doing better at following our Life Compass than we thought. Reviewing our life journey is not just about finding what is wrong.

It is more about discovering what is right and good about us. When we discover what is good and right on our journey, we have a better chance to fix what needs fixing on the journey as we realign our lives according to our compass.

Reevaluate Your Values. As life changes. There are times when we must value changes. As we journey the path of our Life Compass, we encounter changes as we are on our way to our True North. As we encounter these changes, some of our values tend to change. In other words, what we valued earlier on our compass path, we no longer value. This often has something to do with our maturity. As we grow more mature in the vital areas of our existence, we realign ourselves with our new values.

Recommit to Yourself. We make commitments to everything and to everyone else, but the one person we sometimes forget to commit to is ourselves. Life compassing calls for self-Commitment. We will never continue the course of our compass if we never make a commitment to ourselves. When we commit to ourselves, we will not cheat ourselves out of what we deserve. When we make a commitment to ourselves, we commit to accomplishing our dreams and sticking with our purpose as we realign our lives with our compass.

Refocus on Your Purpose. There are times as we attempt to follow the path of our Life Compass, we lose our focus on our purpose. This is human, and no one is exempt. When we lose focus on our purpose, we get out of alignment with our compass. Staying focused on our purpose helps us not go in directions that are leading us to our True North.

Reorganize Your Life. During our life journey, practicing reorganizing on a regular basis is important. There are times when things simply get out of order. Then there are times during our journey when our lives become cluttered with various things. These types of events can knock us out of alignment with our compass. Therefore, as we attempt to follow the path of our Life Compass, we must put forth an honest effort to clear ourselves of the things that cause us to get out of alignment and take actions towards realigning our lives according to our compass.

Reprogram Your Mind. Getting into alignment with our Life Compass has much to do with how we think. If we never get it in our minds that we are out of alignment with our compass, we will never do what we need to do to realign ourselves. Sometimes our old way of thinking does not match where we are in our life journey. When our thinking pattern does not match where we are on the path of our compass, we get out of alignment. Whenever this is the case, we need to reprogram our minds to get to our True North. We must remember that our actions will only follow what is in our minds.

Breaking Old Habits and Starting New Ones

How our lives are aligned with our Life Compass heavily depends on our habits. How we talk, walk, eat, sleep, think, treat others, treat ourselves, as well as our perspective of life and the world is based upon habits we have developed over time. Habits are acquired behavior patterns regularly followed until they become almost involuntary. Some of the habits we have developed are unhealthy in various ways and sometimes prohibit us from following our compass that leads to living a fulfilled life. If life is going to be enjoyable and fulfilled as we make an honest attempt to follow our compass, we must acknowledge those habits that prohibit us from following our compass, break them, and develop new habits that will help us get closer to our destiny. This can sometimes be painful in some ways because some habits cannot be broken without going "cold turkey." Even though breaking bad habits is sometimes a painful experience, breaking them can be accomplished with intention.

Breaking the habits that prohibit us from following the path of our compass is a process. During the process of breaking the habits that prevent us from following our compass, we must replace them with new ones. If our bad habits are not replaced with new ones, we can possibly go back to the old ones that did not work for us.

Breaking old habits without replacing them with new ones creates a void that needs to be filled. No one likes having a void in their life. I suggest the following steps that can be used to break old habits and replace them with new ones:

- *Make a list of the habits you believe are prohibiting you from following the path of your compass. Depending on your habits you may want to keep this list to yourself.*
- *Make a list of new habits that can replace the old ones. It is not enough to simply make a list of what you want to stop and not make a list of what you want to start.*
- *Set a time frame when you will start breaking the old habits and replacing them with new ones. Remember that it is a process that takes time, depending on the habit. This is about goal setting.*
- *Identify ways you will break the bad habits and start new ones. This is about strategizing. As there are bad habits, there are also good habits.*

Keep in mind that breaking bad habits and starting new ones is a process. There will be times when you may experience failures and successes. If you fail along the way, do not beat yourself down. Get up and go at it again. When you succeed in your trying, celebrate your accomplishments.

Changing Routines

To break old habits and start new ones calls for changing routines. What are you doing? Are you doing what you need to do to get you to where you say you want to go? Are your actions in alignment with what you say you want? Are actions helping you manifest your dreams? Are you doing what you should be doing to follow the unique path of your Life Compass that leads to your True North? For some people, the answer to these questions is a solid "Yes." For others, if they are honest, it is a definite "No." Then, for others, there is a "Pause" because they must stop and think about it because they have no clue. We all tend to fit into at least one of these categories at times. Then on the other hand we find ourselves existing in all three – a solid "Yes" – a definite "No" and a "Pause" because we are not for sure.

There are times when we recognize that our routine of actions is not matching the path of our compass. I believe that this has much to do with being stuck at times in "Sameness." "Sameness" is a lack of variety. It is about being stuck in doing the same things repeatedly, particularly in the same manner without any variation in a routine.

Routines can be defined as the customary or regular course of procedures. It can be defined as commonplace tasks, chores, or duties that must be done regularly at specified intervals without varying from them. Such as getting out of bed at a certain time to make it to work on time, getting dressed at a particular time, getting kids off to school and picking them up from school, having family dinner at a certain time, and the list can go on. People who are goal oriented usually operate by some routine. Without having a routine to get things done at specified intervals, we will get off track and not accomplish our goals. Routines are necessary and vital when it comes to accomplishing goals and objectives.

Some people consider routines and habits as being the same. In my opinion, routines and habits are not the same. Habits are acquired behavior patterns regularly followed until it has become almost involuntary. Habits can be performed at times without really thinking hard to do them. They can just happen because they have become part of our nature. Routines take deliberate action towards something with a set goal in mind.

Even though routines are necessary and vital, certain routines can be prohibited when it comes to living a compass driven lifestyle and reaching our True North.

When it comes to living a compass driven lifestyle, we will encounter challenges that demand a change of routine. When I speak of encountered challenges that demand change of actions as we live compass driven lives, I do not speak of these challenges as being negative. Some challenges are positive in the sense that we are pressed upon to try new things that we always wanted to try but was too afraid to try for some reason or another, to go for the dream that sometimes calls for us to break our own rules, and release our untapped abilities, gifts, and starts looking at the world around us from a fresh perspective which can be greatly beneficial. I call these challenges because even though they are not negative, we are sometimes squeezed out of our comfort zones to do these things and we are challenged to abandon some of our customs.

The general definition of challenges is a call or summons to engage something that demands a change of mindset, actions, or patterns. You will discover that as you follow the path of your Life Compass, you will be challenged to change some of your beliefs, the way you do things, as well as the time you do things.

When I resolved to put forth an honest effort to start living compass driven and go for what I believe is my destiny, there were times and even now when I become uncomfortable. This is because I am challenged to change my own rules as it relates to how I used to approach life. As we follow the path of our compass, we discover new things about life, as well as new things about ourselves, and we will be challenged to change the way we have been doing things. Some of our routines over time have become like Linus Van Pelt's blanket in the Peanuts Cartoon. Linus's blanket was what he depended upon for reassurance and comfort.

Our blanket may not be literal, but it can be in the form of routines – routines that give us reassurance and comfort as we do them. However, they can be stagnating. Yes, depending on the routine, they can be stagnating. They can be stagnating in the sense that while we should be using our time, energy, and efforts to move more towards the life we envision, we can spend our time, energy, and efforts at doing things that have nothing to do with where we are trying to arrive at in life. I am not suggesting that we should not have any time for fun and relaxation. Fun and relaxation are also necessary and vital as we are on our compass journey. All work and no play make a dull life.

Some people spend countless hours in routines that have nothing to do with their Life Compass and nothing to do with the type of life they envision. I know this firsthand.

Even though I envisioned the type of life I wanted to live and have the potential to get there, some of the routines in which I was engaged in, even though they were good things and benefited me and others, many of them had absolutely nothing to do with my compass. Once I acknowledged this, I had to do an assessment of my routines and identify those things that were not helping me stay the track of my compass. Changing my unnecessary routines was like pulling teeth because some of the routines I had to change and others I had to simply let go of.

Again, I ask, what are you doing? Are you doing what you needed to do to get to where you say you want to go?

Here are some suggestions that may help you assess which of your routines are necessary and which ones should be changed or abandoned considering your compass:

+ *Reflect on your daily routines, and identify and list those that are necessary that may not have anything to do with your compass but has everything to do with your life, i.e., what you do when you first wake up in the morning, getting kids off to school, going to work, cooking meals, cleaning the house, etc. These things take time out of our day.*

+ *Make the time to identify and list the routines that have absolutely nothing to do with your compass nor push you closer to the type of lifestyle you envision for yourself. Those things that are time and energy wasters.*

+ *Make a list of the things you enjoy doing but may not be directly connected to your compass or your destiny. They are fun and you enjoy doing them. Remember that even though you are compass driven, you still need to find time for fun things. Doing fun things can be refreshing and empowering as we follow our compass path.*

+ *Compose a calendar, a schedule, and strategies to get the necessary things done with less effort and time, as well as the definite things that will complement your life compass. When we schedule things in our lives it brings order. When things are in order, we tend to get things done with less stress.*

Seeing Beyond What You See

To change routines, particularly those things that do not help you down the path of your compass, you must see something worth going for beyond what you see in your present condition of existence. **What do you see? How are you viewing your life and the world around you? What do you see in your future?** Taking the path of our compass and going in the direction of our destiny, depends on realigning our lives according to what we see as being our future.

We will never attempt to realign our lives to our Life Compass if we do not see an alternative reality beyond our current reality. We will never change old unproductive habits and establish new productive ones if we cannot see beyond where we are. We will never change our routines if we do not see ourselves doing better and greater things beyond what we are doing presently.

As I talk with some people, I am made aware of the fact that some people have a deficit of insight. Much of this is because some people cannot see past where they are, what they see presently, and what they have seen with their physical eyes. Some people cannot see new pictures, because they are stuck in the re-runs of their past, as well as being captivated by the gloomy movie of their present.

We sometimes miss seeing greater things, because our perspective is sometimes limited, and we can't see the forest because of the tree in front of us.

One must be careful not to allow what we see in our immediate condition of existence to dictate, determine, or direct the audacity of our insight, vision, and imagination. When we allow our immediate condition of existence to dictate, determine or direct the audacity of our insight, vision, and imagination, we will be reluctant to take the path of our Life Compass and we never take the daring leap towards our True North.

We can be limited by what we see or do not see at times. If we cannot see ourselves being other than where we are presently, we will never go anywhere other than where we are. If we cannot imagine ourselves with more than what we have, we will never have the aspiration that propels us to work hard and invest hard for more. We will simply settle for the limits of life.

So many people are living lives that are sedated and paralyzed by what they see and have seen, to the point they cannot see anything else. Therefore, they take whatever life throws them even though they have the potential for more and to do more. As a result, instead of them taking the challenge to follow their Life Compass to their True North, they settle for what is not to their advantage. Much of this is due to their having physical sight, but a lack of insight. Seeing something with our physical eyes in most cases is simply a matter of opening our eyes. However, seeing something beyond what we see with our physical eyes is a matter of having insight.

Insight plays a vital role when it comes to living compass driven. On the path of our compass, we will see some things that can be discouraging and challenging. If we do not have the insight to see beyond these things, we can easily abandon our compass path.

Insight is an instance of apprehending the truest nature of something, especially through intuitive understanding. When we see something with our physical eyes, we see reality, and sometimes that reality can be a bit scary. What we see with our physical eyes is real. On the other hand, even though we see the reality with our physical eyes, insight helps us see an alternative reality despite the reality. Living a compass driven life and leaping from where we are towards where we want to arrive, eventually takes seeing beyond what we see in our immediate condition of existence via the power of insight.

Here are ways that can help you see beyond what you see:

+ *Do not just take the negative things you see on your compass path at face value. Because something looks a certain way, does not mean that there is all there is to it.*

+ *As you take your compass path find out the truth about what you see before you commit a response to it. Sometimes we respond to things so quickly that we miss the truth about it.*

+ *See yourself taking the path of your compass beyond where you are and you living your best life and doing what you enjoy the most.*

AFFIRMATION #4

I am where I am supposed to be on purpose. I am living according to my purpose. I awake each day, living my life intentionally and not by accident, fate, or luck. I know what I want and where I am going without apology.

Part 4

Acknowledging Where You Want to Go, and Going for It

We cannot arrive at a certain place in life without first acknowledging where we desire to arrive. When we are clueless as it pertains to what we envision our lives to become, the circumstances we encounter in life will choose our destiny for us. One of the most powerful things we can do is to imagine ourselves being somewhere other than where we have been and where we are presently.

Chapter 13
Life Compassing through Imagination

"*The future is not there waiting for us. We create it by the power of imagination.*"

-Vilayat Inayat Khan

"*Imagination is everything. It is the preview of life's coming attractions.*"

-Albert Einstein

Knowing where we want to go and going for it takes imagination. Living according to our Life Compass and finding our True North takes imagination, followed by actions that complement what we imagine becoming, doing, and accomplishing. We cannot arrive at some place in life or even evolve into the unique person we are created to become until we engage in the power of imagining. Imagination helps take the path and continue the path of our compass as we picture alternative realities that supersede our present condition of existence.

I have always been interested in art. Even as a boy, living with my mom and three siblings in a duplex apartment on Frank Street in South Dallas, I was interested in art. It gave me a chance to imagine a world that was not necessarily accessible to everyone. Even though, I grew up with limited choices it did not keep me from loving and appreciating art. Art gave me a chance to imagine a world that had yet to become a reality.

I remember drawing spaceships and strange characters that were a part of my imaginative world. When I was in the eleventh grade, I became more interested in art which afforded me the chance to study art at the Southern Methodist University (SMU), after being recommended for a special program from my art teacher. My first aspiration was to be a studio artist which changed over the years.

I was fascinated with master artists such as Michelangelo, Pablo Picasso, Leonardo de Vinci, Nathan Jones, Arthello Beck, and Alix Beaujour. They indirectly taught me to have imagination. Over the course of years, imagination played a vital role in my life journey. I had no idea that the various components applicable to art, are also applicable to me compassing my life as I desire to live according to my Life Compass. As I set out to live compass driven, I discovered that the gap between imagination in art and the imagination in living according to my Life Compass and staying focused on what I believe is my destiny is narrow. I hope you will discover the same as you set out to live according to your Life Compass and stay focused on what you believe is your destiny.

Many people may assume that there is something magical about imagination and that not everyone can imagine. As a result, some people miss the opportunity to bring life to what they desire it to be.

Imagination does not happen in its deepest and most rewarding sense automatically. As we seek to live according to the path of our Life Compass, we must intentionally imagine alternative realities beyond where we are currently in life. Like a lamp that must be plugged into an electrical socket to ensure that it will give light, the same applies to life compassing. We must plug into our imaginative power to illuminate the path we are to take as we follow our compass and stay true to our True North.

What is Imagination?

We all can imagine. No person is born without the ability to imagine, whether it is through daydreaming or dreaming in our sleep. The difference is that some people use and cultivate their imagination more than others.

With Life Compassing imagination is critical, it allows us to conceive various possibilities of our future and understand our past, juxtaposed with our present, in a way that has real value. Imagination is a fundamental part of our nature. We were created to envision that which has yet to become reality. Even as kids, we imagined ourselves in worlds that were never heard of. This made our lives fun and adventurous without ever leaving the house or the block we lived on. Through childish imagination, we traveled the world without catching a plane, train, or bus, or traveling by car, walking, or running. Just on the wings of imagination, Muhammad Ali once said, "The man who has no imagination has no wings."

One of my hobbies is scuba diving, even though I never lived close to a large body of water that would afford me the luxury of diving frequently. Nevertheless, I love water and always have. When I was young, I used to imagine swimming underwater with the fish as I fought off hungry sharks and explored sunken ships. We are all born with the uniqueness to peep into another world. The problem with being born with an ability to imagine and fantasize is that we grow into adulthood, and we sometimes dismiss our ability to imagine. What a waste of a great God-given gift.

To not waste such a precious and necessary gift, it is imperative that we define imagination. Imagination is the act of forming mental images of that which has yet to become reality but is believable. It is a natural ability to create mental pictures of that which has yet to be experienced materially or physically. Imagination is the image projecting faculty of our minds which consistently paints, sculpture, and design in our present condition of existence, that which has yet to manifest in real time.

Without the use of imaginative tools, our worlds would be dull, mundane, and uneventful to say the least. No man moves from one point to another without first seeing himself in his mind where he desires to be.

Compassing Imagination

We exist in a world full of imagination. We live in an environment empowered by the acts and dynamics of imagination. We are connected directly and indirectly to other human beings and nature, as well as other worlds by the power of imagination.

The use of imagination is important when it comes to living according to our life Compass and staying intentional about reaching our True North. The cliché that says, is correct. We see more clearly in picture form.

Imagination helps us discover our Life Compass, as well as our True North. Unfortunately, some people never live according to their compass because they fail to use the power of their imagination, that they are driven to the point of acting on what they imagine. When we fail to imagine ourselves other than where we are, we will remain where we are. On the other hand, there are times when we imagine being in places other than where we are, we yearn for it so deeply that we go for it, almost by any means necessary. I contend that people who live compass driven lives and stay focused as much as possible on their destiny use the power of their imagination to do so.

Compassing Imagination is using our ability to imagine by which we paint vivid pictures and images on the screen of our minds that helps us see that our present is full of powerful possibilities and that we have a great and awesome future ahead of us as we are intentional about following the path of our Life Compass and remain true as much as possible to our True North. In life compassing, we connect the dots of our past, present, and future that helps us live the type of life we desire and are created for through the power of imagination. In life compassing, imagining is more than fiction. It is about taking the real pieces of our lives and connecting them to create a world full of possibilities.

Sharpening Your Imaginative Tool for Life Compassing

Tools must be sharpened from time to time for them to be effective. The imaginative tool is not exempt. Keeping our imagination sharp while journeying the path of our Life Compass as we stay aimed in the direction of our True North, is important.

Even though we enter this world with a level of imagination, there are those who seem to have a greater capacity for it than others. Whether deep or not, our imagination must be sharpened and cultivated if it is going to do what it was designed to do as we live compass driven.

A sharp imagination helps us look deep within ourselves and identify all that we are capable of accomplishing. It helps us to think outside of the box of familiarity. When we begin thinking outside of the box of familiarity, we can begin imagining ourselves in better places with a great future.

Here are some things we can engage in regularly that can help us sharpen our imaginative tool:

Practice detaching from social media for a certain time. Social media keeps us informed of the happenings taking place around us, or for entertainment, but it sometimes does not help us sharpen our imaginative tool for Life Compassing.

Try just chilling out regularly. Sharpening our imagination for Life Compassing involves shutting out external stimulation and impulses. When we simply take the time to exit the hustle, bustle, and noise, fresh images come into focus as our minds are turned off from the world for a period.

Listen to music without lyrics. When we listen to music without lyrics, the music can boost and prime our imagination, and we have the chance to form our own images and write our own stories accompanied by the music we are listening to.

Read various types of literature. Reading various types of literature offers a colorful pallet from which we can paint various images of the canvas of our minds that can be stimulating as we take the path of our Life Compass.

Engage in a hobby that you do not consider as work. Having a hobby frees us from the hustle and bustle of an average workweek. Hobbies afford a chance to have fun. Fun helps sharpen our imagination. Remember, all work and no play dulls our imagination.

Engage in stimulating and positive conversations. Stimulating conversations that are positive help sharpen our imagination to embrace possibilities. When we engage in stimulating and positive conversations, we are refreshed and encouraged to stay the path of our Life Compass and keep going for our destiny.

Engage in meditation and relaxation. In life compassing meditation and relaxation are important because it helps keep our minds, spirits, and bodies refreshed for the journey as we follow the path of our Life Compass.

Take the time to observe nature. Nature is a master teacher and being in nature or taking the time to observe nature is like having a front row seat in one of the best classrooms ever created. Nature stimulates our own creativity. Life compassing calls for creativity. We cannot create or be innovative without imaginative stimulation.

Coloring Outside the Lines

<u>As we take the path of our Life Compass, there are times after acknowledging what we want and going for it, we will be challenged to take risk of being somewhat odd and get out of the box of average, familiarity, and comfortability</u>. For me, even though I believe that I know what I want for the rest of my life and have the faith and nerves to go for it, I am sometimes tempted to simply stick with what I have and with what I have been taught over the years. I think we all deal with this temptation from time to time. Considering that it is easier to hold on to the way we have been doing things, as well as hold on to what we have been taught. It usually requires no real effort. We can sometimes sit back and let things flow in any direction it chooses. However, when we are inspired to

follow the path of our Life Compass and go for our True North, we will be challenged to investigate and take inventory of the way we have been doing things and what we have been taught. Once the investigation is completed and the inventory has been done, we may discover that the way we have been doing things and what we have been taught does not match where we are in life, and it does not match what we want presently. This can be a bit scary and even uncomfortable depending on where we are in life, as well as our mindset and faith because we are challenged to start coloring outside the line.

I define coloring outside the lines as, daring to live beyond the boundaries of some societal norms – outside of the lines of being average – outside of the lines of our traditional beliefs and school of thought, and outside of the lines of what we are accustomed to doing and familiar with.

Coloring outside the lines may not be all bad, it may be a sign of creativity. Remember your first coloring book, along with the small box of crayons with limited colors. Remember when we were small kids how coloring was fun because we colored with no rules – just creativity, even though the pictures we were coloring was bordered by lines, it did not matter because we were free to use our imagination and add our personal touch with not much regard for the lines. All we knew was that we have a picture to color and the colors to use. It really did not matter who liked it or not, we were just taking advantage of what we were given. A coloring book and a box of crayons.

Those were the days when coloring was fun because we could color without really minding the lines, even though we knew they existed. But, as we grew older, we were taught and almost demanded not to color outside the lines. I understand why, it was to teach us some type of discipline, and perhaps range perception.

We were taught to color with rules – the rules of coloring. After we were taught not to color outside the lines, coloring was no longer the same, it became more about the lines than creativity.

It became an analytical task, instead of being fun and creative. I guess what we were taught about coloring is no different than what we were taught and are still being taught, and that is to never color outside the lines of life – do not break any rules – stick with the norm and stay in the herd.

We are taught as adults that anything that does not fit the average rules of approach – if it does not fit the box – the customs of the day – if it is not logical and fit to flow down our rational streams, it is all bad and can't work or be accepted by society or our peers.

It is no wonder why we have become a society filled with average or below average people. We have forgotten how to color outside the lines. After all, what is faith besides believing that something more exists and can become reality beyond the lines of life that often borders us from becoming all the Creator has created us to be and to receive all we are created to receive?

When it comes to taking the path of our Life Compass and going for what we desire from life, we must accept the fact that taking the challenge to color outside the lines can be scary and uncomfortable at times, it is imperative to do so if we are going to arrive at our True North. It calls for us to break some rules, even if they are the rules, we have set for ourselves over time. It calls for us to use our imagination and our ability to create and redefine things in our lives because sometimes the path of our Life Compass that leads to our True North is not a straight shot. It has curves and bends that demand us coloring outside the lines of our journey.

Chapter 14
Don't Settle for Nesting

"There is no passion to be found playing small – in settling for a life that is less than the one you are capable of living."
-Nelson Mandela

<u>**You will never get what you have acknowledged you want out of life while settling for nesting – where you are.**</u> You have not been created to nest throughout your life while the world moves on around you, and without you participating in the movement. Even though we have not been created with literal wings, we have been created to soar into our great future and arrive at the awesome destiny for which we have been created.

One of the hardest things not to do while following the path of our Life Compass as we are inspired to keep moving towards our True North, is not to give in to the temptation to settle for nesting. But if we settle for nesting, we will never know the amazing things we can do. Vince Lombardi said, "If you'll not settle for anything less than your best, you will be amazed at what you can do in your lives."

Even though I wrote this book, I know first-hand what it is to be tempted to settle, or to give in to just getting by or to simply settle for some golden nuggets, life throws us from time to time. If you can be honest with yourself, you too will admit that you are not exempt from the luring temptation to settle or resolve to just get by or settle for some golden nuggets, life throws you from time to time. Each of us, no matter who we are, are tempted at times to settle and nest even when we know what we desire out of life and even have the ability and potential to get it. It is a part of life, and no one is exempt.

It is easier to settle for nesting where we are in life than it is for us to break the chains of settlement and leap from our nest, spread our wings and soar. It is easier to settle for nesting because nesting calls for no real efforts or planning on our part. When we settle for nesting, we can just let life take whatever course it is going to take, and we can just ride the ripples. But one thing I have discovered, and that is, that usually the ripples never take us in the direction that leads to our destiny. I have also discovered that even though it is easier to remain in the nest and feel safe, we miss some of the greatest and awesome experiences that are available to us. There are some great things, great people, and great experiences we will never get to while nesting. Some of the greatest and awesome things, people and experiences that have been appointed to us, and us to them on our compass journey will not simply show up at times, we must go to them. But to do so, we must be willing to get out of our nest. I have also discovered that even though it is easier to stay in our nests and not to spread our wings and soar, we become stuck in sameness and ruts. Our days look the same, feel the same, and absent of the new and refreshing experiences we need to feel like life is worth living.

When I took a backwards glance at my life journey, I come to the realization that I sometimes gave in to the temptation to be a nester instead of spreading my wings and soar. Even though I could have accomplished more, I settled for just maintaining what

I had and what I had accomplished. When I think about it, some of this was due to fact that I was in what one may call a good place according to societal norms and religious norms. But something in me was never happy or satisfied. Hold it! It was not that I was not grateful for what I had accomplished. I have always been thankful for what God provided for me and my family, but something was missing. I was being pulled by something in a direction that I could not ignore or shake. There was a void that needed to be filled. I realized that I was attempting to fill the void and satisfy my yearning, while remaining in the nest I had chosen to stay in. See, nesting is a choice and not an absolute. We have been given the freedom to choose whether to be a nester or a soarer. My question to you is, which do you choose?

In my present journey as I am inspired to follow the path of my Life Compass and stay focused on what I want out of life, as I maintain my focus on my True North, I must admit there are times when I am tempted to be a nester than a soarer. I am saying this to you because I do not want you to feel as if you are alone in your journey of being tempted to settle for nesting versus getting out of your nesting place and begin to soar. If this is where you are in your compass journey and even if you have not decided to take the path of your compass journey, you are not alone. If no one else is with you, I am with you. We are in this together. We can get out of our nests and soar the path of our compass and keep going towards our destiny together. Together we must realize that the best of our lives is at our fingertips. But we cannot grasp it while settling for nesting.

Do not settle for nesting – do not settle for limitations in areas of your life where there is more – do not get sucked in and comfortable with areas in your life that clip your wings and prevent you from flying, and do not get comfortable with momentary events and people in your life that may prevent you from spreading your wings and soaring.

I define nesting as the following: Settling, Wrongful Satisfaction, Procrastination, and Self-denial.

Settling: Nesting can be considered as having a disposition and attitude of settling. Settling is taking whatever life throws us and making no real attempt to change the course of things. Settling can be distinguished between contentment. Contentment can be defined as having peace of mind in situations that have yet to change. When we are content, we may not be happy about how things are, but we have peace with it to the point that it does detour us off the path of our compass. Contentment is sort of keeping our balance and faith until our situation changes for the better. Contentment is having the disposition and attitude that what is will not always be. On the other hand, settling is when we take the position and have the attitude of "Que Sera Sera, what will be will be, the future is not ours to see." As a result, we fail at practicing the power within us to attempt to alter our present condition of existence, to assure a greater future for ourselves. We will never live our best life in the present nor grasp the possibilities of our great future while settling.

Wrongful Satisfaction: Nesting can be considered as acquiescing to being wrongfully satisfied. Satisfaction is a state of gratitude for what we have whether it is much or less. However, it does not imply that we do not desire more. Wrongful Satisfaction is when we simply become satisfied with the way things are and what we have accomplished while having the abilities and potential and even the opportunity to do more and be better, but we choose to stay in our nest instead of flying. We sometimes do this by psyching ourselves out to the point that we are happy with where we are and the way things are, but underneath we are still longing for more out of life.

Procrastination: Nesting can be considered a form of procrastination. Procrastination can be described as deferring actions towards what is most important or what we should be doing at an appointed time for a certain result. It can also be defined as putting time and energy towards things that have nothing to with what we say we desire out of life, as well as having nothing to do with the path of our compass or our destiny. Procrastination kills dreams, visions, plans, ideas, and inventions. It is an enemy of progression. It can chain us to our past, as well as our present. The chains of procrastination must be broken if we are going to follow the path of our Life Compass and reach our True North.

Self-denial: Nesting can be considered a form of Self-Denial. Self-denial is the sacrifice of one's own desires. It is the instance of retraining or curbing our desires. Self-denial is needed and can be healthy in some cases. There are times when we need to deny ourselves of certain desires, particularly when they are not healthy or rewarding for us. However, when it comes to life compassing and reaching our destiny, self-denial causes us to not award ourselves with what is needed and deserved. When we deny ourselves what is needed and deserved we end up nesting instead of flying. We will never follow the path of our Life Compass or go for our True North when we deny ourselves the permission and privilege to live the life we desire. We just end up nesting.

I have identified several symptoms of nesting.

* *We continue to do the things that never worked, or no longer work for our best benefit, and we become reluctant to attempt and take the risk of doing the things that we know have the possibilities of working f or our benefit.*

* *We tend to use our circumstances as liabilities and make agreements with them to stay where we are versus moving forward to new levels. As a result, we come up with excuses as to why we should remain nesting.*

* *We tend to entertain the impossible more than we entertain the possible. Sometimes without knowing the facts. We will always remain nesting when we do not make the time to investigate the factual possibilities that are available to us.*

* *When we try to fit into something that no longer fits us and cannot be adjusted. It is like trying to squeeze into some clothes that we have outgrown. We may look good in them, but we are uncomfortable and sometimes gasping for breath.*

* *When we fail to tap into our untapped potential. Studies have shown that the average person lives off twenty percent of their potential while letting eighty percent of their potential to go unused or wasted.*

Breaking the cycles of nesting and exiting your nest is totally up to you. No one can do it for you. It is a matter of choice. The question is, will you choose to nest, or will you choose to fly?

Needed Interruptions

There are times that for us to break the cycle of nesting we need interruptions. I do not like interruptions, particularly when it stirs my nest, even when I know that there are some things in my life that need to be interrupted and I have been nesting too long in places that have not been productive and have nothing to do with my Life Compass or my True North. There are times when I prefer for things to stay as they are and not be touched or moved around, particularly when I have arrived at the conclusion that even though things are not their best and I could be doing more than what I am doing, at least they seem to be working and I know what these things are. We get comfortable. **When something is interrupted and my nest is stirred, I am challenged to regroup and consider doing some new things that take me out of my comfort zone, as well as challenge me to spread my wings when I have been used to keeping them folded while I stay cozy in my nest.** Can you relate to such a tendency? Let us face the fact, no one really wants something interrupted when we are feeling cozy in our nest, even when we know that we are not at our best or doing our best while nesting. When we are pushed or pulled out of our nest to fly it can be a bit scary because the unknown has a way of causing a bit of anxiety or stress.

However, even though I do not like interruptions, I have discovered that life requires interruptions to get us out of our nests to fly. I will talk about what it means to fly later in the book. As it relates to taking the path of our Life Compass and staying pointed in the direction of our True North, interruptions are necessary. If some things are not interrupted and they remain the same, we will settle in places of comfortability and familiarity, even though we have been gifted for more, to do more and move forward.

Even though we have acknowledged what we want and are inspired to go for it and follow our Life Compass and move in the direction of our True North, some interruptions are necessary. Even though we know these things and know the path that we are on and should be on, we still give into nesting from time to time.

The purpose of interruptions or the stirring of our nest is to get us in position and urge us to use what we are gifted and equipped with to soar into our best life. We are created to do more and be more, but sometimes we never do what we should be doing until something is interrupted or stirred. I say this from my own experiences. There were times when I became alright with the way things were and with what I was doing at the time, even though I knew there was more in me and that I wanted more. I resolved that regardless that I knew that I had more to give and wanted more, I was going to settle for where I was and with what I was doing. Then came the interruptions and the stirring of my nest. I discovered that there is something about life that will not allow us to live in neutral.

When I started going through the process of my nest being stirred, I was drawn to Deuteronomy 32:11 (NIV) which says, *"like an eagle that stirs up its nest and hovers over its young that spreads its wings to catch them and carries them on its pinions."* After reading this Scripture I became curious about how an eagle stirs its nest. In my research, I discovered that the eagle's nest is made with sharp sticks padded over with down which is under the exterior feathers of the adult eagle. The mother eagle will either shake or pluck the down off her chest to cover the sharp sticks in the nest. This is amazingly comfortable for the eaglets despite the sharp sticks. When it is time for the eaglets to leave the nest because they have developed their wingspan to fly, the mother eagle begins the process of plucking the down from the nest which makes the once comfortable eaglets become uncomfortable, to the point that they must use their wings and fly out of the nest. After discovering this, I came to understand that God by His permissive will was allowing some things in my life to become uncomfortable for me because I had what it took to soar higher. Whatever or whoever your magnetic pull is, you will not be allowed to remain in your nest when your wingspan has developed enough for you to soar the path of your compass. It will keep pulling you to your destiny whether you like it or not.

Have you ever wondered why when things seem to be going well, they become uncomfortable? Have you ever wondered why the comfortable places you found yourself in are no longer comfortable? Have you ever wondered why the successes and accomplishments you made that once gave you joy, and you felt the fire and the drive, but at some point, you found yourself looking for the joy, the fire, and the drive, but was not able to find it? All you know is that you woke up one day wondering what in the hell happened to the joy, the fire, and the drive. And you found yourself in neutral. Not going backwards or forward, just existing and wondering. Did you have a dream that you used to look up to because it was bigger than you and it gave you the challenge you needed to keep making life work? But you arrived at a point in your life where instead of you looking up at your dream, you were looking down at it because you had outgrown it. This is because you have arrived at a nesting place, and you are being interrupted and your nest is being stirred for you to fly into your best possibilities. Sometimes interruptions are exactly what we need to get us out of our nest and start spreading our wings. I have come to realize that interruptions do not come our way for the purpose of destroying us but to develop us so we can take flight, even though we do not enjoy our flow being interrupted.

T. D. Jakes says in his book entitled, *Destiny – Step into Your Purpose*, "Maybe you feel it's time for change in your life. It may not seem like a good time to shift your priorities or start reordering life plans. It may not be the right time to change jobs, go back to school, to move to a new city, break away from an unhealthy relationship, or change your spending habits. That is when God begins stirring the nest, initiating disruption so you will get moving." This can be scary. At least it was for me even though I have faith in God. I came to realize that the nest will not be stirred until we have developed our wings to fly. We just need to trust our wings.

Break Free of Your Nest

When we have encountered needed interruptions, it is a sure sign that it is time to break free of our nest. Cemeteries are filled with dreams, inventions, ideas that could help change the world, books, businesses, and industries, along with gifts, visions, talents, abilities, and potentials of those who left this world without ever breaking free of their nest. This should not happen to you or me. We have a chance to break free of our nest. Do not leave this world with what you can do and accomplish still in you, because you decided to be a nester, versus one who breaks free of their nest.

<u>When I leave this world, I want to leave while I am in flight and not while I am nesting. One of the greatest tragedies of anyone's life is to have the wingspan, the potential, and the opportunity to soar great heights but settle for walking throughout life and never experience what it feels like to soar.</u>

We all tend to fall into a cycle of nesting at times, whether we are on the path of our compass, or not. Nesting is a matter of choice. We have been created to soar. We are free to choose between nesting and soaring. If you have been nesting, you can break free of your nest, whatever it is. The day will arrive when every person must decide if they are going to leave the nest and soar or live the rest of their life on the sharp sticks in the nest after the down is taken away. Either way, a decision must be made. Breaking free of our nest is not just something we do. It is also something we need to do to live the type of life the Creator intends for us to live. Until we conclude that breaking free from our nest is something we need to do, we will always come up with an excuse for why we are staying in our nest and have not taken the path of our Life compass that will eventually get us to our True North. Again, we can break from our nest if we make up our minds and muster up the courage to do it. I have identified several steps that can help us break the nesting cycle.

Step One: *Resolve that you no longer want to continue to nest. If you never make up your mind that you want something or vice versa, you will never put forth a real effort towards it.*

Step Two: *Identify what causes you to nest, i.e., fear, past failures, low self-esteem, procrastination, doubt, mistrust, etc.*

Step Three: *Take the time to think about what your future will look like if you continue nesting. What will you miss? Then take the time to imagine the great possibilities in your future once you get out of the nest. What will you gain?*

Step Four: *Give yourself permission to get out of your nest and begin to spread your wings to fly. Even though you may resolve that you no longer want to remain in your nest, it is imperative that you give yourselves permission.*

Soar the Path of Your Compass to Your True North

It is time to spread your wings and take-off down the path of your Life Compass into your True North! You have the wings to do it! You have been made for it! You have made it to this point in the book. It is evident that you are interested in taking flight. I hope that you are excited about meeting the new you, as well as about the awesome and great possibilities that lay ahead. I am excited for you. You have the wings to get you to all you have been created for.

Even though we do not have natural wings, we have been gifted with abilities, potential, talents, visions, dreams, and ideas that I believe are symbolic of wings because once they are spread, they can take us to new heights, new levels, and into fresh experiences that can change the course of our lives for the better. We just need to learn how to trust them as we soar into our best life.

To soar means several things:

To Soar – To move through life on new heights of our potential and abilities to make things happen that will help us live the type of life we have been built for and deserve. This is not without some difficulties. Whenever we decide that we want the best out of life and we go for it, we will experience difficulties that will seek to clip our wings. But these this can be overcome with faith and the tenacity to keep moving forward.

To Soar – To move beyond and above our unfavorable circumstances and situations. No matter how determined we are to take and stay on the path of our compass and reach our destiny, we will encounter unfavorable circumstances and situations that will try to turn us back. This is inevitable for anyone who desires better for themselves and even for others. But we do not have to allow the winds we face to turn us back. We can keep going if we desire what we want bad enough.

To Soar – To not allow the worst of life to get the best of us. This is sometimes a hard thing not to do because we sometimes believe that we can never get past the worst. Our worst experience does not have to get the best of us if we decide to get the best of our worst. Remember that we have been given what we need to get the best of and out of our worst experiences. Our worst times do not mean that time is out for us to go for the type of life we desire and deserve to live.

To Soar – To spread your wings in new and fresh winds when life is trying to tie you down. Soaring is not without trial and struggle. It is natural for us to stay on the ground, and unnatural to soar. We sometimes allow things to pin us to the ground. We have been equipped to break free of anything and anybody that tries to keep us from soaring into new and fresh winds. It takes faith, courage, and hard work to do it.

Keep in mind that soaring the path of your Life Compass to your True North is not predicated upon your circumstances or past. Soaring the path of your Life Compass to your True North is about who you choose to be, and what you choose to go for. We can come up with all sorts of excuses as to why we are not soaring our compass path, we can even spend time blaming others for not soaring our compass path, and as to why we are not closer to our destiny or as to why we have not arrived at our destiny. The bottom line is that soaring is not based upon our circumstances, neither is it about others. Soaring is up to us. If we want to soar, we can. If we decide to nest, we will. It is a matter of choice. Soarer or nester? We make the decision.

Chapter 15

Taking the Leap

"*A dream coming to pass always requires a leap between what is now & what could be.*"

-Holley Gerth

"*Sometimes your only transportation is a leap of faith.*"

-Margaret Shepard

Winnie the Pooh said to Christopher Robins, "I always get to where I'm going by walking away from where I've been." **We will never know what it feels like to spread our wings and soar until we have the courage and tenacity of "Pooh Bear" to move from where we have been or where we are presently and walk to some edge, of where we are challenged to leap.**

We will never know the reality of what we can do and accomplish until we take the challenge to leap from what we believe is the safety of our nest. The only way we can know our next reality is, by taking the dare to let go of where we have been and move from where we are presently and take a leap into our future. It has been said, "until you spread your wings you will have no idea how far you can fly."

It is said, that when eaglets are no longer comfortable in the nest, or when it is naturally time for them to spread their wings and fly, they get up and make their way to the edge of the nest. I can only imagine how frightening this can be, even with wings. I can imagine the eaglet finally mustering up the courage to stand on the edge of the nest and looking around at the open sky and asking himself "Should I leap, or should I stay?" Then saying to himself, "I know that the sticks in the nest are sharp and uncomfortable, but at least I know what they are. I've been dealing with them for a while. I know them by name. But I am not sure about this open sky thang. In the nest, I have something to grab ahold of. But I do not see anything to grab ahold of in the open sky. So, should I leap, or should I stay and just settle for the sharp sticks. Humm?

I can also imagine the eaglet standing on the edge of the nest and looking down at the ground below and saying to himself, "That's a long way down. What if this wing thang and flying thang is a hoax? What if I am really meant to stay in the nest and not fly, even though I see other eagles flying? What if I leap from this nest and find out that I am not meant for flying but just for nesting? If this is the case, I will leap and hit the ground and that would be the end of it all. Humm? Hard decisions, hard decisions."

Do these scenarios sound familiar? These scenarios are familiar to me. As I had mentioned in the early part of this book, I had made it to a point in my life and family life that was comfortable. I thought that the only thing I needed to do was to maintain the lifestyle I had developed over time. I did not take what I call "Necessary Leaps." "Necessary Leaps" are doing those things that we should be doing to get us from one place to another that makes life work for us. It is facing our challenges head-on, going against the odds, and making the needed sacrifices to get to where we desire to be in life and go for what we want out of life. It is operating in our faith to face our fears and put up a good fight against anything and anybody that stands in our way, that tries to keep us from getting to what we want and believe we deserve out of life.

I leaped, I leaped hard, and I leaped fast. I did not spend much time standing still and letting grass grow underneath my feet. I did this without apologizing for going for what I wanted. After leaping over the years and finally making it to a place where I was comfortable, I contended that I had arrived at the end of my leaping days and years. I was fine with it. I was cozy in my nest. After all, I had spread my wings and soared in skies that only some people imagined.

However, one morning I woke up and came to the realization that I was no longer satisfied with where I had arrived in my life, even though it was a good and decent life. Something was growing in me that I could not explain, or at least I did not want to acknowledge what it was, even though the feeling was familiar. You know how we play mind games with ourselves sometimes, hoping that what we are feeling and know will soon go away. This was not the case. The feeling stayed. It tugged! It pushed!

When I finally came to grips with this feeling–this tug – this push, I discovered that it was another leap in me. One that I did not expect. Again, after all, I was in a good place in my life. Sometimes the good places we are in, in life are not the greatest or the best place. Sometimes we are tugged and pushed to move from good to great and from better to best.

Leaping is not something we do one time and move on. Leaping, I discovered from my own experiences, and not from theory, books, sermons or lectures, and lessons are a lifestyle versus a one-time deal. It is a continuum. It keeps on flowing. When we take the first leap, something is conceived in us and once it is conceived, it desires to be birthed into our whole existence and grow to its fullest maturity and potential.

I was impregnated with another leap and did not know that it was a continuum of my previous leaping. My friends, once we have leaped from our nest, we will be pressed upon to keep leaping as long as we have breath because the wheels have been put in motion. We will be pressed upon to keep leaping in some way or another and from one thing to another. For some of you who are reading this portion of this book, this may be a bit scary. Relax! I assure you from my own experiences that when it comes to leaping and being tugged and pushed to leap again and again as a lifestyle and a continuum, you and I have been equipped to take leap after leap, from the edge of our nest and soar. We have been born for it. We've been equipped for it. It is in us whether we acknowledge and receive it or not. All I know is that when there is another leap in us, in some form or another, standing still and simply trying to maintain is never satisfying and that trying to fit in with nesters makes for a miserable life.

You have made it through this book. You know what a compass is and how it can benefit you as you live the life you have been created to live. You feel the needle of your Life Compass pointing you down the path you should be going. You have an idea of what your True North is, or at least pondering it. You feel your Magnetic Pull firing up the cylinders of your talents, gifts, abilities, and potential. What you have been dreaming of is more real than before, and your imagination is so awesome that you envision yourself entering your destiny and you can see a picture of your best. You are standing at the edge of your nest, and you are probably asking yourself, "Should I leap, or should I not?" "Should I take the path of my compass and go for my True North or just stay the path I am on and pray and hope that life turns out for the best?" If you are feeling like this. I want you to know that you are not alone. Deciding to leap from familiar places and take the path of our Life Compass is not always an easy decision to make even when we know what we want from life, and what we are capable of accomplishing.

Even though we know what we can do and accomplish. We know our talents, gifts, abilities, and potential. Taking the leap from familiar places and beginning to soar the path of the unknown, can be one of the hardest decisions we will ever make. Like the eaglet that stands on the edge of the nest, there are times when we will see nothing in the open sky to grab a hold of, and the ground is far down. This can be scary at times.

Even though we do not like how the sharp sticks, in the nest feels, we can get comfortable with them over time. We have dealt with them over time, and we can call them by name. We know what they feel like. We have dealt with them so long to the point that we become immune to them.

For those of us who desire to be compass driven and follow the path of our Life Compass staying in the nest is not something we entertain the most, even though it comes to mind from time to time. When it comes to leaping from our nest and following our Life Compass sometimes the hardest thing for us to do, is to get the courage to move to the edge. The question is, how do we get to the edge of our nest to get ready to leap and take flight into our new frontier?

I suggest the following when it comes to leaping:

Get to the Edge of Your Old Self

As I think about getting to the edge of our nest and taking the necessary leap to soar the path of our Life Compass and making a beeline to our True North, I conclude that it is not our obstacles, misfortunes, set-backs, problems, or the problematic people we encounter on our journey that gets in the way of something greater. We usually get in the way of ourselves. We will never take the leap and soar the path of our compass and get to our destiny until we allow ourselves to get to the edge of ourselves.

Nothing or no one can really keep us from living the life we are born and designed to live. Nothing or no one is so great that they keep us from following the path of our compass or keep us from our destiny. They can only cause delays, but not denial of the life we are born and designed to live once our minds are made up. The only person that can keep us from journeying the path of our compass and reaching our destiny is us.

Once upon a time in my life, I believed that it was my negative experiences, and the negative people I encountered that were in my way and keeping me from following the path of my compass and from making a beeline to my destiny. After taking a serious inventory of my life, I concluded that it was not negative experiences, or negative people that were prohibiting me from taking the path of my compass and making a beeline to my destiny. It was me. I was my own barrier. I was my own enemy. I was keeping me from my best. Perhaps you can relate. After arriving at this shocking deduction, I realized that if I was going to live according to my Life Compass and get to my True North, I had to get to the edge of myself.

Each of us has an "old self," which makes up our nature, character, ego, and temperament that is often fed by our beliefs. We were born with this "old self" that has grown over time and often goes unchecked because this is who we are used to. However, if we do a checkup on our "old self" we may discover that it may be keeping our "new self" from coming out and from taking the path of our compass and going for our destiny.

There is a "new self" that is biting at the bits to be released, but our "old self" is covering it up and keeping it from coming out. To release our "new self" we must come to the edge of the "old self."

When I arrived at the point of really wanting to live a compass driven life and not just let my life go in just any direction, I had to admit that I had to get to the edge of my "old self," because it was keeping me hostage. Every time I attempted to go in the direction that I knew was best for me, I would be kidnapped by my "old self." My old nature, old character, old ego, and old temperament. My "new self" was never going to be released until I finally came to the edge of my "old self."

Getting to the edge of something denotes that something is coming to its conclusion. It also denotes that something new is getting ready to start. Getting to the edge of our "old self" speaks towards the idea of bringing our old nature, old character, old ego, and old temperament to some end and releasing new ones. When we get to the edge of our "old self" by chiseling it from around our "new self" the new and fresh image will appear, and this new image is the one who is equipped to take and handle our compass and get us to our destiny.

We can learn this from Michelangelo's statue of David. It has been said that for more than two years Michelangelo searched for a block of stone out of which he could create and release the type of sculptured masterpiece worthy of being placed in the main square of Florence.

It is said that one day, while traveling on a familiar dirt road outside of the city, Michelangelo discovered a huge piece of marble, that was overrun by weeds and shrubbery. He had passed this piece of marble dozens of times but never given it any thought. On that day, something was different about that huge piece of marble. Filled with inspiration, the artist had the stone hauled to his studio. There he began the arduous task of hammering, chiseling, sanding, and polishing the old piece of marble, out of which erected the image of the famed statue of David.

You have a "new self" that is ready to appear and take the awesome path of your compass and get you to your awesome and unique destiny, if you will get to the edge of your "old self" by taking on the arduous task of hammering, chiseling, sanding, and polishing until the new image of you is released.

Here are some things you can do to get to the edge of your "old self" and release your "new self":

+ *Take a real and honest look at your nature, character, ego, and temperament to ascertain whether, or not they complement what you believe is your compass and destiny.*
+ *Identify what is keeping you from releasing your "new self." Is it outdated beliefs, habits, fears, religion, the way you have been taught, etc.?*
+ *Take the time to list ways you can get to the edge of your "old self" and begin living according to your "new self."*
+ *Once you have gotten to the edge of your "old self" and started to live in your "new self," celebrate! When something new and great is born, it is worth celebrating. Celebrate you!*

Just Do It!

"Farmers who wait for perfect weather never plant. If they watch every cloud, they never harvest. Just as you cannot understand the path of the wind or the mystery of a tiny baby growing in its mother's womb, so you cannot understand the activity of God, who does all things. Plant your seed in the morning and keep busy all afternoon, for you don't know

if profit will come from one activity or another – or maybe
both." – **Ecclesiastes 11:4-6 (NLT)**

I am always inspired by the Nike slogan, "Just Do It." Even though it relates to a style of sneakers or their brand, it can also be applied to life in general, acknowledging what we want from life.

The idea of "Just Do It" is not suggesting that we throw all caution or even concerns to the wind. But it does suggest that we should be careful not to be so overly cautious in the face of opportunities that we miss them. It suggests that one does not spend all their time waiting for what they deem is a better time before they go for what they believe will become a reality. It does not suggest that we proceed on the path of our compass without a plan or goals in place. It suggests, however, that if we plan, and set goals for our compass, but get off track for some reason or another that we do not quit and abandon our plan and goals but get back on the path of our compass and keep going and moving ahead. The slogan encourages us not to wait before we go for the best that we can be and accomplish, as well as for the best possibilities that are allowed us in life.

Considering Life Compass and finding our True North, the "Just Do It" slogan is about us not waiting until the winds die down and the clouds go away before we plant our best seed and gather our best harvest. We will experience some winds and clouds that will tempt us to either abandon our path or take other paths that we are not designed for, as we are inspired to live compass driven lives. But we must remember that even though we will be tempted at times to abandon the path of our compass or take paths that we are not designed for, we do not have to give in to the temptation, because we have been afforded the power of choice.

In life compassing, winds and clouds are inevitable. They are a part of nature and our journey as we live compass driven. If we do not remain mindful of this absolute, we can become easily discouraged and abandon our path, even though we have acknowledged what we want and even after going for what we want. I know this all too well. For many years I knew what I wanted out of life and even put forth the honest hard effort at going for what I wanted and even began compassing my life accordingly. I had many successes. During my journey, I ended up giving much of my attention to the winds and clouds that came along during my journey. As a result, I was thrown off the path of my compass and I took paths that I was not designed for and had negative repercussions. My attention was also thrown away from what I knew was my destiny. As a result, I allowed myself to be lured to taking the road of least resistance by which I became miserable and unsatisfied. I knew that there was more in me and that I was created for more than what I was doing at the time, even though in the eyes of others, I was living a successful life. Well, we can't really know the content of a book simply by its cover. I concluded that I was way off the path of my compass, and I had lost sight of what really mattered to me, as well as what I knew was my destiny. Instead of "Just Doing It," I stopped doing it – I stopped doing what I should be doing, and I stopped doing me! Simply because I paid more attention to my winds and clouds.

I finally concluded that if I was ever going to live the life I was created to live and love, I had to resolve that no matter how hard the winds blew and how many clouds gathered or how dark my path became, I had to get my life back on the path of my Life compass and be intentional and determined to stay focused at any cost on the direction of my destiny. This is a continual task. And it will be for you if you are going to maintain the path of your Compass and find your True North. Remember that it is not just the strong who survives, but it is also the focused who survive.

I encourage you, that as you are intentional and determined to live according to your Life Compass and get to your True North, do not allow the bellowing winds and the dark clouds that gather while you follow the path of your Life Compass distract you off your compass path to the point that you lose vision of your destiny. For we do not know what will succeed, whether this or that or both. But we will never find out what will succeed if we do not resolve to do what we should be doing, can do, and be good at it.

When we pay more attention to our winds and clouds, instead of living according to our Life Compass and staying focused on our True North, we become reluctant to plant our best seed and bring in our best harvest, and life becomes an unfulfilled journey. Your life can be fulfilling if you "Just Do It."

AFFIRMATION #5

I am leaping into my future with open wings. I will not cheapen my future or sell myself out for a handout, a check, a position or for popularity that will dimmish my quality of being and the quality of my future.

Chapter 16

Conclusion: Your Compass Journey Begins

"Take pride in how far you've come. Have faith in how far you can go. But don't forget to enjoy the journey."
-Michael Josephson

"Start shaping your own day. Start walking your own walk. The journey is yours, take charge of it."
-Dr. S. Maraboli

Y ou have made it to the conclusion of this book, but the rest of your unique, powerful, and awesome life has just begun. <u>**The path of your Life Compass has been laid, and your True North awaits your arrival with open arms**</u>. This can be exciting and a bit scary at the same time. It is exciting in that you can embrace the new you without apology and shame. You have arrived at a place where you can begin writing a new and beautiful chapter to your life book. You are the author who holds the pin. It is exciting because you can begin releasing the things that have been keeping you constrained from moving forward and embracing the life you desire to live. However, it can be a bit scary, because as we take our compass journey all the answers, we desire will not be readily available to us. It can be a bit scary in that, we venture into the unknown, even while knowing what we want out of life and where we desire to arrive. In addition, we will be summoned by voices that will tempt us to take the road of least resistance, off the path of our compass journey. We will face obstacles and temptations that will challenge our going forward. Be not dismayed! If you look deep within yourself, you will discover that you have been born and equipped with everything you need to make your life work. You are enough, embrace it, and live it out loud for the world to hear, and let the light of life shine like the sun that lights ways of others.

In chapter one, I gave you the 7Cs that are the basic principles of this book: *Clarity, Commitment, Consistency, Courage, Conviction, Confidence,* and *Constraints.* These basic principles are not just for the foundation of this book, but they are also basic principles that can be used practically in our daily life and help us stay on the path of our compass. As you begin your Life Compass journey, consider these basic principles as road signs that point you in the direction of your True North.

7Cs of Your Compass Journey

CLARITY – *The clearer you are about who you are, what you really want out of life, and where you are going, the more likely you will live to your fullest, achieve what you want and eventually arrive where you want to be.*

We cannot follow the path of our Life Compass and stay in the direction that leads to our True North without having clarity. I am not talking about clarity in the sense of having all the answers to all our questions. Life does not afford us the luxury of having immediate answers to every question we have.

When I speak of clarity, I am referring to being clear about who we are, what we want, and the way we are going.

Who are you? When it comes to life compassing, it is important to know who we are. We may not be clear about who others are, because people can and will change. However, if we are going to follow the path we are to take through our lives, we must be clear about who we are. We must know our strengths, as well as our weaknesses, our temperaments, dislikes, and likes, as well as what turns us on and what turns us off. Without having a sense of these things, we will attempt to embody someone else's personality which will not work for us as we attempt to live compass driven.

What do you want? When it comes to life compassing, it is also important that we are clear about what we want out of life. I have discovered in my own life, that if we are not clear about what we want out of life we will take anything that life throws our way. Some of the things that life throws at us are not meant for us, because they do not match who we are authentically. When we know what we want as we take the path of our compass, we will know what to say "Yes" to and what to say "No" to.

Where are you trying to go? When it comes to life compassing, we must be clear about the way we are going. We will remain lost or get lost if we do not know where we are going. It is impossible to arrive at a certain destiny if we are not clear about where we are going. Without knowing where are going, we will end up anywhere. Many people live their life in circles because they have no clue as to where they are going or at least trying to go. We may not be clear about everything in life, but we can be clear about where we are trying to go. We are the only person who can choose the direction we go. It is our responsibility to choose the direction we go, regardless of the situations, circumstances, and people we encounter.

COMMITMENT – *Be so committed to live your best life that you sell yourself on yourself, to the point that you make an agreement and a pledge to yourself to never stop going for what you believe is yours.*

Generally, commitment can be defined as the state or quality of being dedicated to a cause, activity, etc. It is an agreement or a pledge to do something for yourself or someone. When it comes to sticking with the path of our Life Compass, commitment is necessary. We can be committed to various things and people, such as jobs, careers, hobbies, religion, charities, relationships, etc. I believe the greatest commitment we must have, is a commitment to self, to make life work and live our best life.

The path through life has many twists and turns, and they can knock us off the track of our compass if we are not committed to ourselves, to going all the way to the destiny for which we are created.

To go all the way to what we are destined for takes more than just being committed to our jobs, careers, hobbies, religion, charities, relationships, etc. To go all the way to what we are created for and destined for starts with being committed to ourselves. Without self-commitment we seldom finish what we have started, and we sometimes fail to stick with giving our best to other commitments. It is almost impossible to give our best to something or others, what we do not have for ourselves. We will never give our best efforts to other commitments, until we have made up our minds to be committed to changing ourselves in such a way that we are committed to releasing out of us everything we have been born and equipped with, to make the type of life we desire and even deserve.

CONSISTENCY – *Keep knocking the hell out of the obstacles that stand between you and your great destiny, until you break through them.*

If you keep hitting something hard enough and long enough, you will eventually break through it.

It is easy to start something, but hard to stick with it to its completion. Particularly when we are being pulled in various direction, and our plates are filled with many tasks that we deem important. There are times when we start something with much excitement, enthusiasm, and fire, but we sometimes discover that during our accomplishing what we set out to do, we lose the excitement, we become less enthusiastic, and what was a blazing fire dwindles to a flicker. This sometimes has nothing to do with us not believing in what we set out to do and accomplish, versus it having something to do with the fact that we fail to be consistent at what we have started. To finish anything in life whether it is a small task or a large task, we must be consistent if we are going to finish what we started. I know this firsthand.

I must admit that during my life I have set out to do some things that I was extremely excited and enthusiastic about and even started them with great fire in my belly and heart, and even shared them with others, but I failed to get them completed. My failure to see these things through and get them completed had nothing to do with poor planning or a lack of confidence or potential. However, it was due to the lack of consistency.

Without consistency, we abort every dream, idea, vision, plan, etc., that was conceived in us. As a result, every dream, idea, vision, plan etc. that was conceived in us will fail to go its full term. Therefore, they are never birthed into the world.

When it comes to living a compass driven lifestyle, consistency is the main ingredient. Without it, we will not stick to the path that gets us to the destiny we are created for. If we are going to reach our True North, consistency must be one of the principles we live by. Without consistency, we will easily abandon the way we should be going to reach the point in our lives where we begin to live out our possibilities.

COURAGE – *Courage is not about never being afraid. It is not about never facing obstacles that seek to block us from succeeding. Courage is about looking our fears in the eye and not shrinking back. Courage is having the tenacity to push through what stands in our way to reach the point of our success.*

Attempting to live a compass driven lifestyle is not lived in the absence of fear. Neither is it done without facing obstacles that seek to block our path to keep us from arriving at the place and point in life we desire to be.

Every person who is inspired and motivated to travel their truest path that will lead them to the type of life they dream of and do the things they are extremely passionate about, must face their fears and deal with the obstacles that seek to border them from reaching their highest level of life. Fears and obstacles are common denominators whether we are compass driven or not. No one is exempt from fears and obstacles.

I used to believe that if I had real courage, I would not and could not be afraid of anything. I also believed that if I had real courage, it would be easy for me to get past my obstacles. I found out that this is not the case no matter how courageous I was. I came to the realization that having courage is not about never being afraid or getting past our obstacles easily.

Courage is usually awakened when we are faced with something that threatens our existence in some form or another. Courage is never needed when we are not encountering obstacles. Courage gives us the tenacity that is needed to face our fears head-on and look them in the eye and refuse to shrink from our deepest beliefs. It is also about being brave enough to stand before our obstacles and dare to keep pushing forward.

When we make an honest attempt to journey the path of our compass and continually go the direction of our destiny, we will encounter events in our lives that cause us to be fearful at times, as well as face various obstacles that stands to prevent us from moving ahead. Therefore, it takes courage to stick with our Life Compass and keep our attention aimed in the direction of our True North. Without courage, we are sure to abandon our path and take the ways of least resistance. We must remember that to give in to our fears and obstacles is to give up on ourselves.

CONVICTION – *A person without conviction will lay down for anything and stand up for nothing. You must have conviction to live your best life. Without conviction, the path you take will be guided by the opinion of others and by what is deemed to be most popular.*

I contend that it is impossible to live our best life without having a conviction about something, particularly when it pertains to a certain quality of life. Quality of life is not based upon how much we accumulate during our life span. The quality of life is based upon the convictions be lived by.

Living by our convictions, in my opinion, is to go for what we deeply believe in without apology or shame. Conviction is not just an attitude, but it is something we believe in deeply.

Convictions are not fleeting thoughts that flit through our minds through the channels of our imagination. Convictions are beliefs we firmly hold to as being principles by which we live by. We must never allow others to sway us from what we believe to be true, and from what we believe we are created for.

We will never reach our point of success and happiness if we rely on the opinion of others versus our convictions. If life is going to be what we imagine it to be, we must hold to our convictions, particularly when our convictions are right and just for all mankind and have much to do with us living the type of life we have been created to live.

We must remember that our convictions are ours, and we must own them and be true to them. When we own our convictions and are true to them, despite popular opinions, our convictions will be true to us, and we will reap the benefits from them in accordance with our pursuits as we take the path of our Life Compass.

When it comes to living according to our compass, having convictions plays a vital role. Convictions are principles and beliefs that help us stay the path of our compass. Even though we may discover our Life Compass and identify our True North, without conviction, we can be easily distracted and swayed from the path of our compass and drawn out of the direction of our destiny by the opinion of others and by what society consider as being normal.

We will never stay the path of our Life Compass and reach our True North without holding firm to what we believe and are convinced to be true for our lives.

CONFIDENCE – *It is not what others believe about us that raises us to our next level. Neither is it about what others do not believe about us that pulls us down to lower levels. What raises us to our next level or pulls us down to lower levels is the confidence we have in ourselves.*

When I speak of confidence, I am referring to self-confidence, which is having a surety of our abilities, potential, skills, mind, qualities, beliefs, judgement, etc. It is about having a positive attitude about who we are and what we are about, without being dependent upon what others think about us or our potential or what they think we are about.

Having confidence is accepting who we are and trusting ourselves while having a sense of control in our lives. It is being OK with our weaknesses, as well as acknowledging our strengths, while knowing that both our weaknesses and strengths are a part of who we are, and we are capable of us using them in a positive manner that makes our life work for the better.

Many people are not failing to accomplish their goals for lack of abilities, potential, skills, dreams, ideas, giftedness, etc. They sometimes fail at accomplishing their goals due to a lack of confidence. Without confidence, we will never pursue what we want out of life, and we will never accomplish what we are capable of accomplishing.

I admit that getting to the place where we have confidence and maintaining our confidence is not easy. Getting to the place where we have confidence is not easy because some of us come from a background that did not promote confidence, versus promoting dependence upon others and upon other things. This is to say that some people are not taught to be strong and independent. They are taught that if life is going to be worth anything, they must be connected to a certain sect of people who make them feel good about themselves. Without them being connected to a certain sect of people they feel worthless. As a result, they never build their own confidence. In addition, some people have gotten caught in the trap of letting their confidence be based upon the accumulation of things, such as money, cars, houses, popularity, etc. As a result, when these things are no longer available or have become less for some reason or another, their confidence begins to decrease. This is due to fact that things and stuff made them feel good about who they are.

When it comes to following your Life Compass and making a beeline to your True North, having confidence, and maintaining it is important. You will discover as you are determined to take the path of your compass, and as you gaze in the direction of your destiny, some risks are involved, and without confidence you will be tempted at times to give up your pursuit for your best life.

While on the path of our compass we run the risk of losing some people we rely on and are close to, as well as run the risk of losing things or having to give up some things. Keep in mind that everyone around us or close to us will not be for us when we really make up our minds to follow our life compass and go for our destiny. The world is full of haters. I have discovered in my own life that some of our haters are in our immediate circle, and if we do not have the confidence that we can make life work, even if we must go at it solo, we will never stay our course of life. In addition, while we are on our compass path, we will discover that we may be challenged to give up some things that are dear to us. Another thing I have discovered as it relates to being compass driven is that we cannot take everything with us on the path regardless of how dear they are to us. There are times when some things must be let go of to reach our next level.

CONSTRAINTS – *Life cannot be lived at its best without limits and discipline. Without constraints, one will say yes to the wrong things and no to the right things. A person without constraints is like a balloon filled with helium and let go in the wind. They will end up anywhere.*

Beyond popular opinion, if life is going to yield its best, it must consist of limitations. Life is less qualitative when we persist in living our lives without constraints. Believe it or not. If we are at all honest, we can admit that no one really like constraints because they have the tendency to make us feel restricted and limited. When we are constrained, we feel like we are being held back from something better or greater. Having constraints can make us feel confined and not free, and we sometimes cite having constraints as being the reason for not being successful, or for not living the type of life we believe we deserve.

However, when we view constraints from a positive perspective, we will discover that constraints help us be successful and live the type of life we desire. The key is looking at constraints not as a negative, but as a positive, as well as it being liberating. It can be liberating in that it frees us up from making choices that are not beneficial as we take our compass journey.

In my personal experiences, I have found that when I had limited choices, time, and resources I was more creative and a better manager of my time and resources. When it came to me getting something important accomplished, having constraints helped me to stay focused and use my time wisely. It kept me out of the trivial traffic and kept me on the true path that I needed to be on to get things done with quality.

I am a foodie. I love cooking. Some of the best dishes I have prepared were made from limited ingredients. I often realized that when I had too many things to choose from, I spent a great deal of time trying to figure out what I was going to prepare. On the other hand, when I had limited choices, it made it easier to make up my mind about what I was going to prepare. So, it is with life and the path we take through life. When we are constrained with limited choices, we have the tendency to be more focused and precise about the choices we make and the way we go.

I believe that constraints in their positive form are important because they help us eliminate what is not important or necessary for us as we take our Life Compass journey. Without constraints, we can be all over the place while attempting to do everything, but not getting anything done that is vital for us.

I have never met anyone who has made it to their destiny or who is living the type of life they have dreamed of living who does not value constraints. Those who value constraints understand the important role it plays in getting them to where they want to be in life.

Constraints can be inspiring. I have learned that when we have limited space to work with, we can come up with unique ways to make the space work. Working within the boundaries of our constraints can bring out our creativity. It pulls out our creativity because it helps keep us focused on the main thing. In a nutshell, restraints help us keep the main thing, the main thing.

When it comes to life compassing, having constraints are essential to our journey, as well as to us. It is essential to our journey in that it helps us stay focused on the path we are on. In other words, it helps us keep our eyes on the road. When we keep our eyes on the road we will know where we are going. We are also able to identify certain obstacles that lay on our path, that can possibly prevent us from getting to where we want to be. Some accidents that occur while someone is driving do not occur because someone is not a good driver. Some accidents happen because some good and capable drivers take their eyes and focus off the road.

Secondly, constraints are essential to our journey in that it helps keep us in certain grooves on our path that make it a little easier to keep our traction. When my family and I first moved to Detroit in the middle 1990's we had no real clue as to how to drive in deep snow. As a result, we would often get stuck. On one snowy morning, I decided to stand at the window to see how Detroiters were maneuvering so well through the snow. What I noticed was that they would position the tires of their car in the grooves that were made prior by the snowplows, which gave them traction. After learning such a valuable lesson as to how to maneuver in the Detroit snow, I became good at it, and getting around in the city on snowy days became less of a hassle, and I did not get stuck in the snow as much as I did prior to learning the lesson. I learned to constrain the tires of my car within the grooves. Our Life Compass acts as the groove we must stay in to get to where we want to go. Without us staying in the constraints of our compass, we can easily get stuck in places that do not promote us to get to our destiny.

Thirdly, constraints are essential to our journey in that it helps us decide on what we will take on our compass path. While developing a compassing lifestyle, we must accept the fact that we cannot take everything or everybody with us, because everything and everybody do not fit the journey we are on, nor promote us to new levels. There were times when I would travel, I would pack as much as I could because I believed that all that I packed was essential for the trip. I soon found out that trying to carry too much stuff on a journey can be costly. On one of my trips, I overly packed my bags as usual. After being dropped off at the airport by my wife. I get at the check in counter and place my luggage on the scale, and there it was, almost thirty pounds overweight, which would have been a bit costly. As a result, I had to call my wife back to the airport to pick up the stuff I had to unload to catch my flight on time. Without constraints, we tend to overpack our lives, which can be costly. However, with constraints, we can choose wisely what we will take on our compass journey.

Finally, having constraints are not just essential to the journey we take, it is also essential to us physically and mentally. In my personal experience, I learned that when I embrace constraints in their positive form, I feel better physically, and was less tired, worn out, and stressful. This is because constraints remind us to not to try to do everything or keep up with everybody. Constraints help us preserve energy because we pick and choose what we spend our energy doing. When we pile our plates with too many tasks, especially those that are not connected to the main thing that we are trying to succeed in, we become overly tired, worn out, and stressful. If we are going to maintain our stability while following our Life Compass path, it is vital that we value our body temple. Constraints are essential to our mental stability and mental health. Mental stability and mental health are about having a balanced mind that leads to balanced thinking that is composed of healthy thoughts. When our minds are not stable and off balance, our thoughts tend to be unhealthy, unproductive, and negative. Practicing constraints help us guard our minds. An unguarded mind usually leads to an unguarded life. When we live a life unguarded, we become vulnerable to almost anything that comes our way, which lures us off the track of our Life Compass, by which we run the risk of never arriving at our True North.

Without constraints, we become like a dry leaf caught in a high wind, that goes where the wind takes it, and we end up in places and doing things that are not complimentary to the type of life we are created to live.

Epilogue

Y ou have finished this book. What you have read is not from theory, but has been birthed out of my personal experiences, as well as tested in my life laboratory.

I hope that what you have read will inspire you to go for your best life and will be an awesome blessing to you as you venture down the path of your Life Compass that will lead you to your True North. I hope you are excited. I am excited for you.

I have given you formulas, beliefs, and practices that I believe will help you live the great life you are created and gifted for, as well as deserve. Yes, you deserve to live a great life no matter what your past has been, even where you are presently. You have a great future in front of you.

I wrote this book out of a sincere heart and a deep desire to help myself and you stay on the path that leads to a better way of living. It will give me great joy to know that this book has helped you through your life journey. I passionately believe and am confident that what is presented on the pages of this book will help you as it has helped me while compassing through this book.

My friend, we may never meet in person, but through this book, we are connected. Our stories are not that much different. They are just written and come to life in different places, and at different times. So, as you take the unique and awesome path of your Life Compass, know that you are not traveling alone. So, stay encouraged and stay pointed in the direction of your True North. See you at the top!

DONALD RAY HUDSON

Afterword

L ife has a way of coming at you fast! Sometimes it knocks you clean off your feet. Other times life carries you wistfully with the wind. Some days are bright while others are long and dark. We all have good moments and unfortunately not-so-good times. Without alarm or announcement, life comes at you fast, and in the blink of an eye... Life Compass. It comes full circle, returning to the way it was, or the way it is supposed to be. Life Compass. It comes full circle, revealing that while good will not always be good, neither will bad, mad, or sad.

But the good news for us, and what I recommend for you is found, right here in this book. *Life Compass: Finding Your True North*. Through detailed explanations, practical tools that will immediately impact your life, and provocative questions (compass prompts) giving way to reflection, Dr. Hudson has shown us how to find our destiny: our True North. We cannot allow our feelings to freeze our future. Feelings are fickle, not final. Remember, we cannot go for what we won't first admit to.

At some point, we all must move beyond the bitter, to the better that lies ahead, no matter how long it takes, but we must allow the Life Compass to be our guide. *Life Compass: Finding Your North* is a journey. This book is developed for a purpose, but achievement takes place in the process. If you've even been through a process, you know that reaching the goal does not happen overnight. Sometimes you must work while you wait.

We cannot control what happens to us, nor can we ultimately dictate what happens around us, but we have a great impact on what happens within us. This impacts cyphers from the decisions we make and the direction we take. That's what separates the good from the great: decisions and direction. Careful decisions and clear direction combined on the journey to find your True North.

What we do with where we are and where we have been determines where we go. What we do with who we are and who we've been dictates who we become. What we do with what we have and what we've lost is a deciding factor to what we gain. It's about perspective, how you look at what you see. And to me, that's the journey of finding our True North.

Here, Dr. D.R. Hudson has laid a pathway for reaching your full potential with the perspective of following a Life Compass, explaining the purpose of our pains while pointing us towards the superpower within us. We're all searching for our destiny, headed in a direction, but not all of us have made the decision to make the most of the moment.

There is more within us than we can imagine. We must be willing, while we're waiting, to simultaneously search for better. Find your True North. Set your mark and reach for your destination.

–Northern Bound

Appendices

"The biggest commitment you must keep is your commitment to yourself."

-Neale Donald Walsch

You have made it to the conclusion of this book. You are impressive and ready for a great and productive present and future. It is my hope that you have received knowledge for living a compass driven life that leads to your unique destiny. However, knowledge without commitment is futile. Therefore, I encourage you to make the decision to follow your Life Compass and go for your True North by committing to yourself and signing the following SELF-COVENANT AGREEMENT.

APPENDIX 1. A

SELF-COVENANT AGREEMENT

I, _____ [your name here], covenant to myself to do my best to live my life according to my Life Compass, and press towards my True North which is my destiny for which I am created. Because I love myself so much that I want all the good things that life has to offer me.

By making this SELF-COVENANT AGREEMENT, I am acknowledging that as I follow the path of my Life Compass and stay focused towards my True North, I will be a light and an instrument to help others connect with their highest self, as I seek to do the same.

By signing this SELF-COVENANT AGREEMENT, I am admitting where I have been, and I am accepting it without shame or apology, I am accepting where I am and own it, and I am acknowledging where I want to go, and I am going for It.

I acknowledge that this is a life-long SELF-COVENANT AGREEMENT that should never be broken and shall be continued by any means necessary.

Signature: _____

Time: _____

Date: _____

COMPASS PROMPTS

The purpose of these Compass Prompts is to help you establish and maintain balance as you take the path of your Life Compass which will eventually get you to the wonderful life for which you are created. These Compass Prompts exercises are based upon certain topics from certain chapters of the book which I believe sets a foundation for a compass driven life. These are mind and soul-searching exercises. It will take imagination, faith, and discipline. As you engage in the prompt exercises, relax, and allow your mind to flow freely. Your responses do not have to be precise or complete. You can always go back to them and alter them as you see fit.

Remember that life compassing is not a race. It is a journey. In addition to the Compass Prompts, I recommend that you get a copy of the *Life Compass: Finding Your True North Journal Workbook*, which offers additional in-depth exercises that parallel with the major point in each chapter of the book.

(Record your response to the Compass Prompts on a separate sheet of paper and keep them for future reference as you take your Life Compass journey.)

APPENDIX 1. B

PART 1
What is Life Compass

Chapter 1
Living Compass Driven

Compass Prompts

1. Take the time to reflect and write your description of your Life Compass. Your compass is yours. You can describe it in ways that fit you best.

2. From your perspective what does it mean for you to live a compass driven life? What do you envision as the benefits of living compass driven?

3. As you begin to pattern your life based upon your compass, what can you begin implementing that will help narrow your path that

will help you become more compass driven? Consider the four points of narrowing your path presented in this chapter.

4. As you evaluate your options, take the time to list the options that can help you maintain your compass path and help you get closer to your destiny.

5. Which route are you presently taking in your life – the valley route or the mountain route? Why? Consider the 7Cs.

6. Do you consider your life as balanced, if not, why? What throws you off balance? How can you become more balanced and even maintain balance? Consider the four points of balance presented in this chapter.

7. What can you begin implementing that will help you stick with the process of your Life Compass? Keep in mind the five points for sticking with the process presented in this chapter.

Chapter 2
Finding Your True North

Compass Prompts

1. How do you describe your "True North" – your destiny? What does it look like for you?

2. What do you believe is your purpose in life?

3. What can you start doing to live out your purpose to reach your destiny and begin living the life you truly desire?

4. How do you describe yourself as you engage in Self-Admission? Try to answer this question without considering how others describe you.

5. What do you need to start taking charge of for you to become more compass driven?

6. Do you know the direction you are going, if not, why not? Is the direction you are going getting you closer to your destiny? How can you be more intentional about the direction you want to go in?

7. As you follow your Life Compass, how can you own more of who you are?

Chapter 3
Your Magnetic Pull

Compass Prompts

1. What or who do you consider as your "Magnetic Pull"? Our Magnetic Pull is the power source that pulls us towards our destiny, as well as helps us stay on our compass path.

2. From which place or perspective of your condition of existence are you living? Are you living from your outer being or from your inner being?

3. What steps can you start implementing that will help you begin living from your unique inner being?

4. What do you believe is your calling? Our calling usually connects us to our deepest passion. What are you deeply enthusiastic about?

5. What ways can you embrace your passion more? Consider the eight points of passion presented in this chapter.

6. Make the decision to put forth an honest effort to engage in "Soul Restoration."

7. Compose a plan to start practicing restoring your soul regularly. Remember that soul restoration does not occur automatically. Consider the 4Rs of Soul Restoration given in this chapter.

Chapter 4
Intentional Changes

Compass Prompts

1. What necessary changes do you need to start making to start living the life you dream of?

2. Change is not always automatic if we are going to live our best life possible. Consider composing your goals for positive change.

3. Identify the areas in your life where you need to persist harder in to reset your life.

4. Make short-term goals to reset in the areas you have identified.

5. Make the decision to start streamlining your life that will help you get balance and maintain your balance as you follow your compass path. Consider the 7Rs of Streamlining given in this chapter.

6. Start thinking of practical ways you can begin enlarging your thinking pattern in a positive manner.

7. If you are being overcome with doubt, identify the source of your doubt, and compose ways you can begin squashing them. Consider the points concerning doubt given in this chapter.

APPENDIX 1. C

PART 2
Admitting Where You Have Been and Accepting It

Chapter 5
Facing Your Facts

Compass Prompts

1. Sometimes facts are hard to face. Instead of lingering on the negative facts of your life, begin identifying your positive facts and begin celebrating yourself.

2. Even if it is painful, take the time to reflect on your story, as well as reflect on your successes.

3. Decide this very moment that you will accept your story, as well as be thankful for your story without shame or regret.

4. How do you feel about your failures? Why do you feel the way you do about your failures?

5. Since failures are natural, what ways can you use them for your benefit?

6. If you could choose between what you are presently doing, i.e., job, career, ministry, etc., or do something different, what would you choose? What is keeping you from making the choice?

7. What is the "One Thing" that if you could get it or begin doing it, would change the rest of your life for the better? Compose a plan to get it, or do it?

Chapter 6
Stop Punishing Yourself

Compass Prompts

1. Do you punish yourself for something in your past or even in your present? Take the time to name the things you are punishing yourself for, even if it is painful.

2. Compose simple and practical ways that will help you to begin to move forward through the practice of Self-Forgiveness.

3. What are the buckets you are carrying and need to drop that prohibit you from living your best life? Consider the five points of dropping buckets.

4. Decide that you are going to put forth your best effort to drop the buckets you are carrying. This may take some help. However, do not be ashamed to ask for help.

5. Make the decision that you are going to start accepting yourself or start accepting yourself more, even if others do not accept you for who you are. Consider the five points of accepting yourself.

6. Take the time to list your uniqueness. For example, "I am unique because …"

7. Take the time to compose "Self-Affirmation" phrases that you can post somewhere and view them regularly that remind you of how unique and wonderful you are.

Chapter 7
Bouncing Back from Disappointments

Compass Prompts

1. Make the decision to no longer allow your disappointments to have power over you, no matter the source.

2. Bouncing back from our disappointments is not an easy task, neither is it automatic. Therefore, take the time to compose a simple and practical strategy that will help you bounce back from your disappointments. Consider the seven points given.

3. Sometimes when we do not identify why we should do something, we never accomplish what we need to do. Therefore, compose a statement as to why you should overcome your disappointments.

For example, "I must over my disappointments because I will be more pleasant to others."

4. How can you become more resilient? Consider the four points on being resilient.

5. As stated in this chapter, there are some things we can't get over, but we can get past them. What events in your life that you have yet to get over that have a negative impact on your life?

6. Come up with simple and practical ways that will help you move past what you can't get over. Consider the five suggestions offered.

7. Start imagining your life without you holding on to the things you can't get over. What does it look like?

Chapter 8
Measuring Yourself

Compass Prompts

1. How do you measure your worth? Are you measuring your worth by your accomplishments, circumstances, or by others?

2. Depending on your answer to the questions above, why do you measure yourself by the things mentioned above?

3. What can you realistically start doing to break this depleting habit?

4. Have you lost your "Cadence – Rhythm"? Why?

5. Depending on your answer to the question above, how can you regain your "Cadence-Rhythm" and start living according to your own beat?

6. What is your purpose?

7. How can you begin living more compass driven?

APPENDIX 1. D

PART 3

Accepting Where You Are and Owning It

Chapter 9
Self-Clarity

Compass Prompts

1. Take the time to compose ways you can become clear about yourself. Self-Clarity is important for your compass journey.

2. What keeps you from seeing yourself clearly?

3. Make the decision to start embracing the true you. How can you be more authentic?

4. What can you start doing to stop concentrating on what you believe is impossible for you?

5. What will your life look like if you start embracing your possibilities? Consider the list given.

6. Make a list of your negative "What Ifs" and plan to break this cycle of thinking.

7. Make a list of your positive "What Ifs" and start putting forth honest efforts to start living according to them.

Chapter 10
Life Detoxification

Compass Prompts

1. What does "Detoxification" mean to you as it pertains to your life and you following your compass path?

2. What do you need to detox your life of? What do you need to start doing to detox your life?

3. Make the decision to start implanting the four steps of "Mental Maintenance."

4. What do you need to be intentional about ending that will help your life to be better and more enjoyable?

5. What have you been spending time and energy apologizing for that really needs no apology? Consider the list given.

6. If you are constantly apologizing for something that can be corrected, make the decision to correct it and move on.

7. What unnecessary weight are you carrying? Decide today that you are no longer going to carry around unnecessary weight. Consider the points given.

Chapter 11
Self-Inventory

Compass Prompts

1. Make the decision to spend some quality time with limited interruptions to engage deeply in Self-Inventory.

2. If possible, find a space with limited interruptions as you engage deeply in doing your Self-Inventory.

3. Doing Self-Inventory takes quality time and reflection. I do not suggest that you attempt to engage all the inventories mentioned in this chapter in one day. Engage each inventory in intervals.

4. With pen and paper begin writing your notes as you follow the suggestions and instructions that are listed under each inventory.

5. After you have engaged each inventory separately, compose a plan to make the necessary changes as it pertains to each inventory where it is applicable.

6. After you have completed your plan of action, schedule some time to reflect on how well you have carried out your plan of action.

7. As you continue your compass journey practice doing a Self-Inventory regularly.

Chapter 12
Realigning with Your Compass

Compass Prompts

1. How well does your life line-up with what you believe is your compass path and destiny?

2. As you consider realigning with your compass, follow the six suggestions listed.

3. Take the time to honestly reflect on the habits you need to break that may be prohibiting you from following your Life Compass. Consider the instruction given. You may want to write these down and keep them private if necessary.

4. Take the time to think about and write down new habits that can replace the old ones that will help you follow your Life Compass.

5. No one breaks a habit automatically. Therefore, compose a plan to break the old habits and start new ones by following the suggestions offered in this chapter.

6. What routines do you need to break, start, and develop that will enhance your compass journey? Consider the list given.

7. As it relates to "Seeing Beyond What You See," take the time to write a sentence or paragraph of what you envision in your future. Let your mind flow freely while being realistic.

APPENDIX 1. E

PART 4
Acknowledging Where You Want to Go and Going for It

Chapter 13
Life Compassing through Imagination

Compass Prompts

1. How is your imagination? Is it limited or is it wide and free flowing?

2. How are you coloring outside the lines of your life? Do you try to stay within the limits and within the boundaries of average?

3. What keeps you from allowing your imagination to run wide and free flowing?

4. Take the time to engage in imagining your life according to your Life Compass.

5. If you are having trouble imagining, compose practical and realistic ways you can sharpen your imagination that will help you on your compass path as you move towards your God given destiny. Consider the eight ways to prompt imagination offered in this chapter.

6. As it relates to your destiny, how do you envision your future, i.e., What type of relationship will you have? What type of home will you live in? Where will you spend your vacation?

7. Make the decision that you will begin composing the life you imagine.

Chapter 14
Don't Settle for Nesting

Compass Prompts

1. Are you settling for nesting instead of putting your best effort forward to soar into your destiny?

2. List the reason or reasons you have settled for nesting instead of soaring.

3. What can you start doing to break your cycle of nesting?

4. How do you view the interruptions in your life? Do you see them as being opportunities to better your life or something that tries to keep you from living your best life?

5. How can you begin using the interruptions that occur in your life to help to begin soaring towards your destiny?

6. What does it mean for you to begin soaring in your life?

7. When you begin soaring the path of your compass what do you envision yourself doing?

Chapter 15
Taking the Leap

Compass Prompts

1. How do you define "Leaping" from your perspective?

2. Are you afraid of leaping?

3. What is it about you that is keeping you from taking a leap into the life you desire to live?

4. What will help you take the dare to take the leap you need to take that will help you get to your God given destiny? Consider the four points given in this chapter.

5. From your perspective, what does it means to "Just Do It"? What do you really desire to do?

6. What is keeping you in your comfort zone, and from not pursuing what you really want?

7. What can you start doing that will help you move beyond your comfort zone and just start doing what you really want to do?

Chapter 16
CONCLUSION: Your Compass Journey Begins

Compass Prompts

1. What do you need to be Clearer about at this point in your life?

2. What do you need to be more Committed to at this point in your life?

3. What do you need to be more Consistent at in your life at this point?

4. What do you need to build your Courage at this point in your life?

5. What are your Convictions at this point in your life?

6. What areas in your life do you need to have more Confidence in at this point in your life?

7. What areas in your life do you need to practice more Constraints?

About The Author

W e are born with a Life Compass that can lead us to the destiny we are born for. Dr. Donald R. Hudson has made it his quest to follow the path of his Life Compass.

Dr. Donald Hudson was born in Texas. He grew up in Dallas Texas, where he received his child-hood education. After graduating from High School, he studied Architectural Design at the El  Centro Community College in Dallas. After studying Architectural Design, he worked as an Architectural Designer in Dallas.

He later began studying for the preaching ministry. He is a trained, licensed, and ordained minister. He has received degrees from several colleges and seminaries. He has a Bachelor of Arts Degree in Biblical Studies and Counseling from the Criswell College for Biblical Studies in Dallas, Texas, as well as a Master of Divinity degree and a Doctor of Ministry degree from the Samuel Dewitt Proctor School of Theology at the Virginia Union University in Richmond, Virginia.

He has taught as an Adjunct Professor for Advance Preaching at the Ecumenical Theological Seminary in Detroit, Michigan. He has also taught as an Instructor for the Study of Black Preaching and Theological Studies at the Heritage Center for Religious Studies in Detroit, an extension study program once associated with the Ashland Theological Seminary in Ohio.

Dr. Donald Hudson has successfully served as a Senior Pastor in Goochland Virginia, Omaha Nebraska, Detroit Michigan, Indianapolis Indiana, and Dallas Texas prior to him retiring from the local pulpit. He has planted churches in Indianapolis and Dallas and has been instrumental in helping plant Mission Churches in Congo Africa. He currently inspires and motivates people via Motivation 4 Impact Ministries which is a virtual ministry of which he is the CEO.

Dr. Hudson is a humanitarian. He has served in foreign missions in several countries and has trained missionaries, preachers, pastors, and teachers in various locations in Africa and Jamaica. He has also been instrumental in helping start a Medical Clinic in Congo Africa. He has a passion for feeding the homeless and those who need sustenance.

Dr. Hudson is a trained Chaplain in CPE (Clinical Pastoral Education). He has severed as a Staff Chaplain in the areas of Oncology, Palliative Care, Heart and Vascular, and in the Emergency Department for Clinical and Pastoral Leadership.

He has spoken from stages and pulpits in and outside of the U.S. He has lectured and conducted Clinics and Workshops on Preaching, Public Speaking, and Teaching Techniques, as well as lectured and taught about Homiletics with an innovative approach, at Preaching Conferences, and National Conventions. He is the author of several books, Sermonic Connection: Simple Steps Linking the Sermon from the Pulpit to the Pew, and Echoes of Inspiration – Journal Thoughts.

Due to him having served on several social, educational, and faith-based community organization committees and boards, as well as having inspired and motivated people from all walks of life, he has received numerous awards and citations from Governors, Mayors, Council Persons in the state of Michigan, and Indiana. He is married to Leatrice H. Hudson. They are the proud parents of two adult daughters and the proud grandparents of two granddaughters.

Dr. Hudson believes that people are created with potential and possibilities that can take them to new and rewarding levels of life experiences when they embrace their authenticity and follow the path of their Life Compass which will eventually get them to their True North, which is their destiny.

Connect with the Author at LifeCompass@yahoo.com